CREATIVE WRITING ENERGY

Tools to Access Your Higher-Creative Mind

KIM PETERSEN
CATHERINE EVANS

CONTENTS

Title Page	v
Acknowledgments	vii
Dedication	xi
Introduction	xiii
Meet Kim Petersen	xvii
Meet Catherine Evans	xxiii
1. Energy: Prayer of Protection	1
2. Unlocking the Power of Your Imagination	4
3. Nourish Your Body, Nourish Your Mind	9
4. Meditation is Sexy	14
5. Mindfulness; as Sexy as Meditation	19
6. Mindfulness is Stone Cold Sexy	22
7. Time-warp & Dreamtime: The Answers are in the Past	26
8. The Pendulum for Writing	33
9. Working With Oracle Cards	40
10. Crystals and Gemstones for Writing Sparkle	46
11. Using Tarot Cards to Explore the Mysterious Mind	49
12. Runes and Writing	57
13. Creativity is Love	62
14. Connecting with your Higher Creative Self	68
15. Xavier Eastenbrick	72
16. Soul Purpose & Connections for Creativity	74
17. Creation and Creativity: A Radical Change in Perspective	81
Afterword	85
Resource List	87
About the Author - Kim Petersen	91
About the Author - Catherine Evans	93
Sign up for weekly inspiration	95

CREATIVE WRITING ENERGY

TOOLS TO ACCESS YOUR HIGHER-CREATIVE MIND

KIM PETERSEN &
CATHERINE EVANS

Creative Writing Energy: Tools to Access Your Higher Creative Mind ©
copyright 2019 Whispering Ink Press

All rights reserved under the International and Pan-American Copyright Conventions. No part of this book may be reproduced or transmitted in any form or by any means, electronic or mechanical, including photocopying, recording, or by any information storage and retrieval system, without permission in writing from the publisher.

Warning: the unauthorized reproduction or distribution of this copyrighted work is illegal. Criminal copyright infringement, including infringement without monetary gain, is investigated by the FBI and is punishable by up to 5 years in prison and a fine of $250,000.

This is a Whispering Ink Press book brought to you by Whispering Ink Press.

eBook IBSN: 978-0-6485491-1-6
Paperback IBSN: 978-0-6485491-2-3
Edited by Paul Vander Loos
Cover Art by Paradox Book Designs

ACKNOWLEDGMENTS

Kim

Never get used to playing it safe. I love this phrase, and I can honestly say those words very much apply to this book. If Catherine and I wanted to play it safe, this book never would have made it into fruition. Playing it safe would have meant us avoiding discussing some of the following topics at all costs. After all, there is a certain stigma surrounding the realm of "new age" thinking and we've gone ahead and applied this thinking to our creative writing. Moreover, we've begun recording a YouTube blog series to go along with this book. Talk about pushing the comfort zone.

Never get used to playing it safe.

For those souls that have crossed my path, enriched my life and inspired me, I am humbly grateful. These are folks that push the boundaries and think outside the box. People that are not satisfied with the ordinary and definitely don't play it safe.

In Catherine Evans I have discovered someone who never says "no" to my crazy ideas. Who is passionate and open to exploration and willing to travel along uncharted territory. A risk-taker and visionary – a kindred spirit. What would I do without her ears, words, patience and time? I cannot express words enough for the love that exists within me for our ongoing creativity, brainstorming and projects. She is an amazing woman, fun to work with and has fast become a treasured friend.

I have known Blair Stewart for about four years. During that time, he and Jimmy – a Vanuatu Healer existing in the higher-realms – have become some of the most special beings to have ever touched my life. Blair continues to act as a solid mentor and trusted friend in my life. It is his encouragement and faith in me that keeps me diving in and exploring new ideas. His vision of me and my capabilities is a notion I strive to fulfil. Without his support and love, I'm uncertain how far my courage might extend.

Xavier Eastenbrick may seem like an elusive online presence to some. I crashed into his inbox late year and he hasn't been able to shake me since. There are not enough words to express the gratitude I have for this very special man. Through his generosity and kindness, he has brought me to tears on more than one occasion. Whether it has been through the wise words he so readily extends to those in need, the hundreds of wands he lovingly creates by hand for sick children, or "just chewing the fat" on the phone and allowing me to keep him up till midnight New York City time, his patience and faith in the world is limitless; and so is my admiration for him.

I want to thank Judy Sweeney for her beautiful heart, her bright light and integrity, and for taking the time to contribute some important words to *Creative Writing Energy*, helping to layer the fabric of this book.

To the path, the universe, personal experiences, and the heart and soul connections that have added richness to my life, offered profound lessons, support and claimed moments forever etched in time, my appreciation knows no boundaries. Nor does my love. You know who you are.

And to you, dear creator, for allowing these words to find you. May you create with love in your heart and continue to uplift the world with your creativity. Never get used to playing it safe.

Kim xo

Catherine

This book would never have come about without my fortuitous meeting with Kim. Thank you to the South Coast Writers Centre, Wollongong Writers Festival, and to the stars and planets for aligning. This is the second book we've worked on, and they just happen. Kim's the air that fans my fire. We have an idea, and next thing it's happening. We're laughing at each other and life, even as we're working our butts off to meet our crazy goals and deadlines. I've never worked like this, and it's exhilarating. Thank you for sharing this with me, Kim. You're amazing.

My parents, Jim and Sue, instilled a great grounding and fed my enquiring mind. For that, and many other gifts and learning, I'm grateful.

My poor husband has put up with me delving into erotic writing and now spirituality. I'm sure he scratches his head and wonders what he's got himself caught up in, but he's there, at my back (hiding). Thank you for your amused tolerance of my craziness.

When I approached other creatives to request permission to

use their work, I never expected the joy, happiness, and thrill I'd receive from their replies. Every person I asked responded in such a positive manner, I was blown away. Thank you, Jodi Cleghorn, Stephen Aidan, Allyson Williams-Yee, Sharlyn Hidalgo, Marie White, and Beth Seilonen. It's no wonder your creativity inspires me!

It's an absolute joy to work with Patti and Paradox Book Covers and Formatting. Her covers are amazing. Thank you for an inspiring cover, with elements for so many more creations.

Thank you to these amazing souls who read my early messy drafts and gave feedback for which I'm ever grateful. Thank you to Paul, who edited such a rough draft from me. I hope to be more organized in the future.

To all who've walked with me along my life path, or crossed it, or shared any part of my journey, thank you for opening my eyes, imagination and mind.

And to my left brain that's struggling with this creative life and writing this book, thank you for relaxing and trusting the right brain, most of the time!

DEDICATION

To those who search for more, those who aren't afraid to look in the shadows, and all who share a creative journey.

INTRODUCTION

Unlock the creativity that exists within you and open your mind to new ways of thinking and being.

It takes a particular type of person to not only write a book but to persist at it. Creative writers are a legion of people belonging to an idiosyncratic faction obsessed with storytelling. We are slaves to the written word; vessels of passion striving to convey our message through story and craving to uplift and transport our readers to other worlds. We are the individuals who function between long bouts of solitary hours living in our heads and real life, and we persist because we love telling stories.

When the moon has aligned and your muse is dancing beneath the stars to the beat of your fingers as they pulse along the keyboard, life is glorious to the writer. But what happens when you glance up and notice that the moon has shifted, your muse has abandoned you, and the steady tempo of words becomes a fading memory?

You know what I'm talking about. I've been there – my muse has skipped out and left me lurking in a place devoid of inspiration while the moon has forsaken me beneath a swathe of thick

INTRODUCTION

wordless clouds. I've experienced those discordant moments as I've desperately scoured my mind in search of prompts and ideas that have eluded me. But I am a writer. You are a writer. We can't just hang around twiddling our unmanicured thumbs waiting for the muse to return and the moon to hang just right.

These are the moments when we realize that we cannot always rely on the muse or the moon to get creative. Therefore, we need a back-up plan – one that allows us to explore and engage our imaginative resources dwelling in the creative realms.

Within the pages of this book, *Creative Writing Energy: Tools to Access Your Higher-Creative Mind*, it is our intention to present a range of alternative methods and ideas that you can use to access your higher-creative mind, which is that part of you that remains hidden and unexplored, brimming with story ideas and characters you have yet to meet.

There is an underlying urge to tell a story for every writer. It's like an invisible pull on your subconscious mind that you don't realize is there until you quieten your thoughts, sit with the feeling and listen – and when you do, something else begins to happen. Suddenly, you're writing the words and your entire being rejoices in a delicious explosion of delight and wonder. Tiny, zealous tingles burst through your body, bringing you to a place of knowing and confirming that now is the moment you had awaited – You are a storyteller.

Wouldn't it be awesome if you possessed the tools and mindset to foster and nurture those inspirational bouts of creativity into something more reliable?

As you move through this guide, feel free to email questions to us. We don't have email handlers or virtual assistants running our email accounts. We respond directly to all emails.

Please send your query and/or comments to:
creativewritingenergy@gmail.com

INTRODUCTION

We can't wait to share with you the methods we use to get creative and stay creative. Are you ready to smash away those invisible writing blocks for good?

You are?

Awesome! Let's get into it!

MEET KIM PETERSEN

Our creative and spiritual paths are intertwined and different for us all. A breakthrough or an awakening can occur beneath the most unlikely circumstances or when we least expect it. It can happen like an earthquake; shattering the invisible boundaries of our lives in a violent eruption. Or it can take effect like a slow drip; layering across the surface of our consciousness as we gradually open our minds to new ideas and new realities.

A magnificent black crow is perched high on my neighbor's roof antennae as I write these words. His jet feathers shine like licorice beneath the afternoon sun as he arches his neck and assumes a proud position, his raspy "kraas" sounding like cryptic messages echoing across the valley.

I look up to gaze at him and smile. His presence at this precise moment is not lost on me. I feel a sense of gratitude that of all the birds to inhabit this valley, it is the crow that has chosen to visit me in this moment. The crow is a spirit animal associated with life's mysteries and magic. The spirit power of this bird is to guide us, provide insight and the means of supporting our intentions.

Many years ago, I wouldn't have noticed a crow screeching

obnoxiously above me. In fact, I might have found it irritating. But now I am aware that our feathery friends are much more than winged creatures that grace our skies. I have learned that birds act as messengers from the other side and symbolize the beauty of spiritual growth. Thus, here I am, about to write an introduction about me and how I've found myself writing a book with my friend Catherine about reaching into our higher-creative minds to tell stories. The gift of the crow's presence is fitting.

The slow drip. The wake of an earthquake produces a steady regeneration of life. The same is true in the realm of spirituality and creativity – it is an unending process of reaching and learning, finding resonance and understanding before reaching some more.

Religion was not a prominent theme throughout my upbringing. My folks didn't go to church on Sunday mornings, or attend Easter mass like other members of our extended family. There were no bibles in our home; no religious deity that I was forced to follow. I learned about biblical teachings during scripture class at school and I hated every minute of it. Funnily enough, each of my own children feel the same way about their scripture studies at school. My father rejects religion. He believes it to be a false set of beliefs designed to exert control over and condition the masses. His strong renunciation of all religion meant that I was free to explore and form my own ideas about spirituality without the pressure of an existing doctrine in my life.

And explore I did.

My mother's mother was part Polynesian. Her fascination with her islander roots leaned toward the darker side of their core beliefs and practices. She filled her home with voodoo totems, pickaninny dolls and black witch symbolism, and she delighted at her grandchildren's obvious discomfort with her decorative tastes.

Although I had been too young to understand the meaning behind the ominous ornaments adorning my grandmother's home, I couldn't mistake the inevitable unease that had accompanied me when visiting. A disturbing energy accompanied her and her belongings, to the extent that I unknowingly became accustomed to the existence of other forces or entities in our world.

Those early experiences with my grandmother and her allure toward voodoo and black magic did more than frighten me. It was those visits that provided the cornerstone for an insatiable desire to seek out the unknown and explore the mysterious aspects of life. Although I hadn't been able to see any ghosts, spirits or entities during my visits there, I *had* been able to feel them. If I could do that, then I knew there were many more layers to exist in this world than meets the eye, and that if there was *darkness*, there was also *light*.

Those elements of the dark versus the light are essential from a creative writing standpoint. Stories were woven around this fundamental theme for eons and continue to provide the foundation for the hero's journey, horror and thriller adventures, fantasy and science fiction as well as romantic tales. We thrive on them as a society and our readers can't get enough.

The fact that you've picked up this book and are reading these words probably means you can't get enough either. There is something profoundly beautiful about being a storyteller. Something important. We are the type of people who like to question everything. We look toward our environment, our lives and experiences to inform our writing. More importantly, we turn toward our imaginative resources to extract the best of our creative flow.

In my later years, I went on to explore the practices and beliefs of Paganism. I came across a little white magick shop in Warners Bay, a small town on the banks of Lake Macquarie in northern New South Wales where I recently moved with my family. I was drawn toward the mystic-looking shopfront brimming with things like handmade wands, cauldrons, crystals and all kinds of wonderful Wicca tools. I then began to stop by the store to explore its offerings and submerge myself in the energy.

The women there had names like Cinnbarr and Moheli and welcomed me into their fold with kind smiles and open hearts. It was during this time that I attended one of their workshops and learned about the pendulum. I have used the pendulum ever since. In fact, when I began writing books, I soon adapted my pendulum practices to help me with my stories.

As lovely as those Wicca women were, I didn't hang around too long. While the spiritual traditions based on a reverence for nature and the polytheistic beliefs surrounding Paganism resonated with me, I didn't fit squarely into their clan. I took what felt right and rejected what didn't. I pondered their beliefs and internalized the information before moving on.

I have spent time studying the history, properties and uses of essential oils, earning a Certificate IV in Aromatherapy. I have quenched my interest in human behavior and studied toward a BA in Social Studies (Psychology) and began creative writing studies. Yet, while I have enjoyed expanding my knowledge in these various areas, it wasn't until I spent a year vigorously studying *The I Am Discourses* that I realized that I had reached the place I had strived toward my entire life. *The truth*.

This volume of books is a culmination of spiritual teachings that are not for the faint hearted. They are not based on any one set of beliefs, rules or doctrines. It is simply the truth penned into words for those who are ready to know them. Despite this, I found myself rejecting and rebelling against some of the teachings. My headstrong tendency to question and challenge knows no boundaries, even when confronted with the only teachings to ever produce a resounding "knowing" at my core level.

I mention *The I Am Discourses* because encountering these teachings were a profound moment in my life, adding rich revelations along my "slow dripping" journey. When the first book arrived at my doorstep and I unpacked it from its parcel, I remember holding the book against my heart, raising my chin toward the afternoon sun and closing my eyes. I was immediately overcome with a sense of déjà vu accompanied by a strange vision and feeling. I knew then that every moment of my life before that had led toward the moment that I would know the pages of that book.

Have you ever experienced that feeling as if the gears in your mind had slipped perfectly into place to produce a dazzling moment of clarity? Those gloriously fleeting moments in our lives remind us when we're on the right track. This path eventually led me to meet the wonderful woman who is the co-author of this book.

Through these *Discourses*, I realized that the light I had pondered as a child when visiting my grandmother's creepy home really did exist. Moreover, through meditation and deliberate practice, I was able to shed invisible boundaries and access other realms as real as the world I view through my physical eyes. Here in these other dimensions we can enter our higher-creative minds.

I know what you might thinking – "woo-woo" right?

But before you dismiss this knowledge as mystical conundrum, I want you to take a moment to contemplate this:

Imagine the intricate layers that make up your mind. When we consider that cognitive neuroscientists claim that only 5 percent of our brain is conscious while the rest lies beyond our awareness, that leaves the vast space of our brains uncharted. That is a seriously mind-blowing observation that begs the question: For what purpose does this exotic area of our brain exist?

I believe this area of our brain remains a mystery for a good purpose. It exists as a dynamic space for the soul to occupy and act as a conduit, bridging our connection to the higher realms and to a higher intelligence. This is the part of our brain that thinks in the expression of form such as images, memories, underlying desires and creativity. It is also the part where we can discover the pathways that lead us to glorious realms – the highest part of ourselves that defines our existence; the obscure and mystic higher-creative mind.

Unlocking your higher-creative mind and crossing the threshold into this magical inner realm is where you can tap into that mysterious space within you and transcend into the creative zone of the higher planes. This is your domain for creating and manifesting; the place where your story ideas thrive along with your imagination and wait for you to channel inspiration.

Putting it like that doesn't sound too "woo-woo" does it?

Catherine and I have come together to bring you something different and special. What you're about to read is nothing new. These mystic beliefs and practices have been around since the dawn of time. We are here to simply remind you that everything you wish to create; every bout of inspiring creative energy is already within your reach and available to access anytime – within the mystic realms lingering in your higher-creative mind. And we're going to show you the pathways to get there. Read on if you're a storyteller ready to unhinge your thoughts and discover alternative ways to enrich your stories. *Creative Writing Energy: Tools to Access Your Higher-Creative Mind* is for those writers who are ready to explore the extraordinary.

Before we dive into some of the methods that we use to enter these transcendental realms, we must first take a quick look at imagination and explore how this magical resource is much more than a means to tell a story. As you'll discover, it is the cornerstone of all creation.

Love & Light,
Kim xx

MEET CATHERINE EVANS

I have a case of imposter syndrome. Have you suffered from that? When you don't feel qualified, not sure that you have anything to offer, and/or aren't certain that you have any 'authority' or 'credibility'. I have varying degrees of this with almost everything I do, and I keep working towards growing out of it.

This is what I'm telling myself: I've been writing all my life, and writing for publication since 2006, so I must have learned a thing or two. I've been involved in Romance Writers of Australia since 2008, and I've immersed myself into learning about genre fiction and the romance genre. I've tried self-publishing, am print and digital-first published. I've participated in lots of writing courses, and even run a few. The other me, Cate Ellink, has published more stories and has explored different territory to what Catherine does. With this book, I'm merging both parts of me and sharing my experiences of life and writing. Maybe that's the terrifying bit!

I grew up in Sydney, Australia, with a conservative, middle class, religious and spiritual upbringing. It was religious in that I was raised in the tight confines of the Catholic Church, but spiritual in that there were some rather dynamic, progressive thinkers around me (including some in the Catholic Church). Asking questions is a fundamental part of my nature, and luckily, I had a lot of people who answered. As an active kid involved in lots of activities, I was exposed to many people who had different beliefs to what we had, but there was always respect for others. It was the perfect ground for my enquiring mind.

In high school, I studied Comparative Religions and it was incredible. There were so many connections and common threads, but it baffled me as to why there were so many differences, sometimes small. I decided that it was because of mankind. Humans, with their incessant quest for power and control, had broken away from a core belief system and tweaked things to develop their own belief systems, creating 'empires' that crowded the world with 'religions'. This decision opened my mind. What was this ancient core belief system? What did I believe?

Sometime after school, when I still lived at home, I decided Paganism was my thing — because of the deep connection to nature, which I felt was integral to the ancient core belief system. No one rejoiced at my diligent searching. Instead, I was told that while I lived under that roof, I was Catholic. Now, I identify with no religion, just beliefs.

My spiritual quest has never ended but has never been center-stage either. Exploring and dabbling, questioning and querying, has been something I've always done. Nature remains the base of my belief, and I'm guided by intuition and energy.

I'll try to explain what I mean by that. Many years ago, I went to visit friends in Jamaica, and they took me to the home of a noted voodoo practitioner, but I couldn't go near the house. I was keen to learn about this incredible practice but the energy I felt was strange, and my intuition told me not to go there. In hindsight, I was too inexperienced and naïve to learn about voodoo. I was overwhelmed by other things.

Timing.

Nature has taught me there's a time for everything. If it

doesn't feel right, then the time isn't right. It doesn't mean you can't do it again later; it's just not right for now.

Now, I find myself writing this book with Kim. The time must be right because for years I've been messing around with many and varied thoughts, blog posts and projects, and suddenly it's come together. Easily. Simply. Spontaneously.

Life's like that — or mine is! I seem to do a heap of unconnected things that feel right. I keep doing them, unable to see how it all comes together. And then BAM! It happens. The timing is right, and the universe shows me how all the little pieces connect into a whole. Do you ever have that feeling?

Writing has been like that. I've always tried to understand my mind by writing down my thoughts. I've always written, even if it's not always creative writing. I had a long sojourn into science where creativity was drummed out of my writing. Facts were the focus, devoid of emotion. I still wrote non-science things, but I became less focused on the emotion in writing. It's certainly what I've found hardest to relearn.

A heap of life events including the beginning of a chronic illness, between 2002 and 2005, caused a speed bump in my life and a directional change for my career. This new creative life is quite the opposite of my earlier science career. In 2010/11, a few things linked spirituality with my creative writing. I wrote a story I called *Past Lives*. I didn't know much about reincarnation, but a story flew from me. I thought it was incredible and took it to a writing workshop where I discovered it wasn't. I decided to 'fix' it and began to research the belief system around reincarnation.

I enrolled in an online writing course with Mary O'Gara. She and her friend had set up an online writing course academy with romance writing classes taught by published authors run out of America. I took many of her classes, because I connected with her, even if I wasn't sure how the class could help me.

I didn't realize at the beginning but I learned over time that Mary had an enquiring mind, a deep belief in the spiritual, and incredible intuition. Mary died a few years ago and I miss her random emails and classes, but mostly her vast knowledge and generosity.

Meeting Kim feels like when I met Mary — fated. With Kim I've found someone else who wants to understand things, who dabbles in everything, who's creative and passionate, interested and interesting. It's like it's meant to be.

Writing is a rather solitary, isolating process where you're inside your head, often with no windows and no easy way out. To write authentically, you need to tap into your innermost self and delve deeply into your psyche. This isn't easy. When you're alone in a fictional world, sometimes you can lose yourself or lose track of your innermost thoughts. Sometimes you're at a time in your life when you run into a Mary or a Kim, and you can connect and work your way out of your head, opening your creativity and clearing your mind. But what if you're alone? Lost? Caught up and not sure how to find guidance?

We've pulled together various practices that have helped us dig deeper, release blocks, find a way out of our heads, and/or find new ways of creating. There is nothing tying these to any belief system. They may be spiritual but are not connected to any religion. They are tools to access your mind, to help you think outside the proverbial box. Not all will resonate with you, but I hope that you'll find a few things that will help expand your mind and help with your Creative Writing Energy, like they've helped with mine.

Catherine xox

ENERGY: PRAYER OF PROTECTION

Kim

Socrates: *"Energy, or soul, is separate from matter, the universe is made of energy – pure energy which was there before man and other material things like the Earth came along."*

Reality is stranger than we think. It's stranger than most people *can* think. And the reality is that everything is energy, including you. Science today accepts that the universe – including us – is comprised of energy, not matter. This is not actually new – it was posited by Greek philosopher Socrates and by the ancient rishis in India thousands of years before that.

Quantum physics states that as you go deeper into the workings of the atom, you see that there is nothing there – just energy waves. Furthermore, an atom is an invisible force field that emits waves of electrical energy or vibration. This means that each moment of every day we are constantly emitting vibrations.

If you are feeling positive, you will vibrate at a high frequency. When you are in a negative state of mind, your vibration mirrors that frequency and will only serve to bring you further down.

Considering the knowledge that we at our essence are vibrational beings made up of pure energy, then it is not a far stretch to believe in the energetic creative resources available to us. Those incredible realms are filled with your creative flow and waiting for your discovery – but before you practice propelling your own energy to merge with these creative dimensions, it is wise to surround yourself with protection.

One of my most treasured friends is Blair Stewart. Blair is a gifted psychic medium who uses various methods such as clairvoyance, clairaudience and clairsentience to receive messages from the other side. He always reminds me of the importance of surrounding myself with protective light because he says my energy is "open". This means I am receptive to other energies – people's as well as unearthly energies lingering in other realms.

When discussing this book with Blair, he said to remind you of the importance of using a prayer of protection in the form of a visualization before embarking on some of the practices discussed and outlined in this book. I advise you to humor Blair and go ahead and just do it. Not only does he appreciate humor but I promise you, if anything, practicing his short prayer of protection each day will raise your energy to a brilliant mass of white light and make you feel better, lighter. What could be better than that?

Kim.

Blair's Prayer of Protection

"I pray to the God guides and the Divine Angels for Divine protection, Divine harmony and Divine love to come into my life."

Visualize: Bring the Divine universal white light through the top of your head then bring it all the way down to your feet. Make it brighter, then push it out around you – at least a meter above and below. Then, fill the light bubble full of Divine universal loving pink light. You must feel the light and the loving energy encompassing you. You then can put the loving pink light through and around others. This is unconditional love, and work. But always do yourself first.

About Blair Stewart: Blair is a credible and reputable member of Bob Olson's Best Psychic Directory. He is a renowned psychic medium, energy healer, and Reiki master who focuses on positive life directions and relationship guidance.

"I tune into your spirit guides, guardian angels and loved ones that wish to communicate with you. Your guides and loved ones may wish to advise you on your present or future circumstances, pass on messages of love, and validate that they are 'alive and well' and still with you in the spirit form. I am not in charge of who comes to communicate with you but ensure to describe who is with you, helping to guide you on your journey."

Blair's Website: https://www.blairstewart.com.au/

UNLOCKING THE POWER OF YOUR IMAGINATION

Kim

"Imagination is more important than knowledge. Knowledge is limited. Imagination encircles the world."
- Albert Einstein

Every now and then, I am drawn into another realm, a wonderous and boundless kingdom where the only factor limiting the possibilities is the scope of my thoughts. I don't need to go anywhere physically to enter this other world. I could be sitting on my outdoor lounge beneath the sun, or at the beach digging in the sand with my children as they play near the shore. I could even be punching the letters on my keyboard, just as I did when producing this article. It doesn't matter where I am or what I'm doing, I always have access to this rich and magical endowment that I can channel anytime and anywhere I choose – my imagination.

Our imagination is one of the greatest gifts we are given and it is as intertwined with the beautiful mystery of life as the certainty of the sun rising at dawn tomorrow. We can't touch it or taste it, and we can't hear it or smell it. There are no scientific analytics or mathematical formulas to support its existence, yet we all know it's there – the invisible thoughts lifting us up and transporting us to other places.

It is imagination that forms the cornerstone of ingenuity. It is essential for the continued evolution of humanity and it is the foundation of all creation.

In his series of texts in *The Marriage of Heaven and Hell,* the 18th century intuitive poet William Blake made this wry comment: *"What is now proved was once only imagin'd."* As you consider the simplicity of these words of wisdom and allow them to seep into your essence, your imagination will begin to kick into action.

Take a look around. Everything you see and all you experience with your physical senses emerged from somebody else's imagination. For something to exist in this world, it must first be anchored firmly into your imagination. Without this perpetual resource, life becomes stifled and creativity is halted.

During his lifetime, Blake was largely considered an outlier for the mystical undercurrents expressed through his creativity – and that's a nice way of putting it. Yet Blake is now recognized as a seminal figure in the history of poetry for his rich symbolism that embraces imagination as "human existence itself".

However, William Blake wasn't alone in his radically insightful views. Throughout the ages, virtually all spiritual teachings speak of the power of imagination; and that invisible formless realm has been bestowed upon you as your birthright.

Our lives today mostly encompass a combination of fast-moving experiences strung together by a series of innovative moments playing out on the leading edge of existence. These are exciting times where revolution appears commonplace, in the form of the technology infiltrating every field from fast food to finances. We're closer together yet further apart thanks to the internet, and each generation contends with profound social, economic and technological transformations.

A fast-track life with the world at your fingertips can often mean a ceaseless internal merry-go-round spinning around the edges of your soul. It can be overwhelming and stressful, and sometimes we lose sight of the important stuff like love, sacred connections and that beautiful essence peering out from behind your cagey eyeballs.

So, while you're taking that look around at everything that was once in someone else's imagination, ask yourself if you've neglected your own. Have you left it at the threshold of adulthood to gather the dust of the passing years? Or perhaps your deadlines have highjacked it along with your mortgage repayments.

Maybe. Maybe not.

No one could blame you if you have temporarily misplaced your wild imagination. We are in an age swamped with selfies and Instagram, little Tweets here, and bigger Tweets there. Did someone mention Snapchat? Yeah, I just heard the teenager throw me some backchat.

What's new?

Your entire life is probably now chronicled on Facebook and you just must keep up with the latest cat memes and viral diarrhea – right?

You'll also need to remember to pay your bills on time, feed your kids after dance class, follow the rules, and for heaven's sake – who let out the damned cat? Catch a little Netflix before bed. You may manage something more, if you last that long, because you're so tired working your butt off to meet the responsibilities that are mounting up somewhere around your hairline, that you feel like your brain will begin to emulsify through your ears.

Meanwhile, you have convinced yourself that it's completely normal for your eight-year-old to watch adults play with *Kinder Surprise* toys and *Frozen* figurines on YouTube just so you can grab a quick five minutes alone and gather your whirling thoughts.

Okay. I might be exaggerating a little. Maybe that scenario doesn't exactly apply to all of us, or all the time. The point is, most of us are so busy, our childlike imagery often becomes a distant memory we seldom entertain, excluding those *Kinder Surprise*-playing-grown-ups on YouTube, of course.

In his wonderful book, *Wishes Fulfilled*, Wayne Dyer says, "*Today, quantum physics confirms the universe is made up of formless (spirit) energy, and that particles (that is, things) do not originate from particles.*" Meaning everything springs from something akin to your imagination. Everything.

Think about that for a moment. I bet while contemplating those words something deep within you recognizes the truth. It certainly gets my inner-bells chiming, especially when considering this observation made by the father of quantum physics, Max Plank: "*Science cannot solve the ultimate mystery of nature. And that is because, in the last analysis, we ourselves are part of nature and, therefore, part of the mystery that we are trying to solve.*"

I don't know about you, but when I first read those words something unfurled and soared through my being at the realization that science cannot take us through the doors of the divine, no matter how hard we knock. The truth is we are as mysterious and beautiful as life itself, and the power of creation is within all of us. It's within the places you choose to take your thoughts, and the ideas that seemingly spring from nowhere. And it lives, thrives and breathes through our stories.

Beneath my author name that appears on the banner on my website is the tagline "stories that transcend". I chose that phrase because I believe story is the perfect instrument in which to nurture the endless creativity of imagination, and I believe it is through story that we can help make the world a better place.

It is particularly true that through fantasy and paranormal storytelling that authors can transport readers to other worlds brimming with magical wonders and spectacular ideas – stories born through the creative forces of imagination that provide an outlet to escape from the demands of modern life as we begin to consider the "what if?".

Yet, as we ponder the magnificence of stories and imagination, and the escapism they provide to our busy lives, there's something more at play here. It's a golden opportunity to snatch back those moments when you dressed up in your favorite super-hero costume and flung yourself off the garage roof; or to reclaim those times when you lost yourself in a world of make-believe that felt so real, you couldn't quite figure out the difference between the parallel realities. Nor did you want to.

So, as you turn the pages of a great fantasy, paranormal romance or sci-fi book and immerse yourself in the characters, a tiny spark ignites the dormant embers of your own imagination, in turn reminding you of your own childlike imagery.

Then something happens – the story ends.

Once you've read the last line and your fleeting visit to a fictional world has come to an end, you're often confronted with the reality of your life. The enchanting tendrils of fantasy begin to fade as the weight of the "real world" sets in. Too soon does the inspiration of a great story merge with the internal merry-go-round until it's lost somewhere in the gray matter of your brain.

But what if you chose to hold on to that feeling? What if you internalized it just a little longer until you have convinced yourself for a few magnificent moments that anything is possible? And what if you danced with the galaxy twinkling beneath your rational thoughts till your essence soared like the inner-child playing make-believe?

Reading the words strung together to form a story created by someone else's imagination, unknowingly gives us permission to unleash our own. But it's when we really take the time to ponder this greatest of gifts that we realize the limitless possibilities that abound in us.

Through the mystical chords of imagination, story will help save the world. It is through transcending beyond your daily responsibilities and releasing *your* imagination that you will expand and enrich your own life.

Imagine that?

NOURISH YOUR BODY, NOURISH YOUR MIND

Catherine

"Instead of thinking of food as the enemy, allow yourself to enjoy the process of planning and preparing meals or going out to lunch with a friend. Stay in the present moment and understand that the purpose of food is nourishment." – Susan Albers

For years I've suffered with post-viral Chronic Fatigue Syndrome, and one of the most frustrating effects is 'brain fog'. Being unable to find words, unable to think clearly, is demoralizing. I've discovered that nourishing my body nourishes my mind and, for me, this means I need to look after my sleep, exercise, food and water intake, and my boundaries.

I'm no expert, in fact, I've got my training wheels on! I'm learning by trial and error. I suspect it's something you need to work out for yourself, because I don't believe one thing suits everyone, even though that seems to be what society believes and pushes.

What works for me may not work for you, but I'll share what I've found and please adapt it to your individual needs.

Sleep: I need a good eight hours. If I don't get it, then I need to catch up. If that eight hours is broken or disturbed, then I need longer. My deepest sleep time is between about 2am and 5am. If I'm disturbed during those hours, I'm not a happy camper. As well as sleep restoring me, it's also time when I can dream, solve problems in my manuscript, and come up with new ideas. Often before I go to sleep, I think about my story, where I'm up to or where I have an issue. I drift off to sleep thinking about it. I have a notepad beside my bed and if I wake up with an idea, I scribble like a mad woman, capturing those thoughts before they dissolve. Sometimes it's rubbish but often it's a clever way out of a problem. Sometimes it's a new story idea. A message from my problem character. It amazes me how busy my brain is while my body rests.

Exercise: I'd always been quite sporty (useless, but sporty) so I never consciously thought about exercise or my need for it. Then I moved to a small town where none of the sports I played were available. It was okay when I worked outside, but when I moved into a more desk-bound job, I found out the hard way how important exercise was to my physical and mental health. When my life became stressed, without exercise there was no outlet for my emotion. The more stressed I became, the less I managed to leave my desk, the less exercise I got, and the more stressed I became. It was a vicious cycle that eventually got me when I became too sick to function. Not the recommended way to learn that lesson. It's been a long road back to being able to do simple exercise like walking, swimming, and practicing yoga.

Writing is such a sedentary job. If I'm stuck with my story, it's often because my body has become stuck to the shape of my chair and I need to get up and move. Circulating the blood seems to wake up my mind. A walk can do wonders for unblocking ideas and words. If you prefer to run, run like the wind and let fresh air fill you with words, ideas, and stories. Get moving, in whatever way you can, to loosen up those creative juices.

Food: If I listen to my body, it usually knows what I need to eat. I love fruit and vegetables. Eating seasonal produce makes sense to me and my body seems happy with light salads in summer, more earthy vegetables in winter. If I eat a lot through the day, I'll happily snack on something light in the evening.

That was easy when it was only me but then I had to cater for someone who didn't share my ideas about food. In my eagerness to be a 'good wife', I stopped listening to my needs and over-compromised. Processed foods, big cooked meals, and foods I wasn't so happy to eat made their way into my diet. I didn't notice this for quite some time. Then I had an ankle injury and was housebound. After two weeks my fresh supplies were depleted and I had to rely on my husband to do the shopping. I asked for healthy meals. He returned with frozen fried rice (there are vegetables in this) and frozen battered fish (fish is healthy). I rang a friend and asked if she could drop me in a salad. My husband had a comprehensive shopping list next time he shopped.

If I'm not eating fresh fruit and vegetables daily, my body and mind deteriorates. I'm not sharp, I feel bloated and awful, tired with no energy. My husband eats an apple a day and that's the only fresh food he requires for living. He could live on processed foods and not put on weight. Over the years I've realized that I need to eat what I require, even if that means cooking different meals. I've learned to listen to my body again, so I eat what I need.

My body sometimes tells me to give stuff up too, and slow learner that I am, I've had to get sick before I faced reality and stopped eating whatever was harming me. I miss some of those foods, but the pain and physical illness they caused makes them highly undesirable.

Water: I need water, lots of it. I'm lucky because I crave it, so I have no difficulty drinking enough. I'm also addicted to tea (black, white, green, herbal, chai, any tea at all!) but there's a limit to how much I can drink, and then I need water. I spent many years working outdoors and the guys I worked with didn't go anywhere without their big water bottles. Even on cold days, we worked up a sweat and had regular water breaks. I was lucky to learn such a great work habit. When I'm hydrated, my mind works well, I feel alert and I have to take regular breaks.

Boundaries: This is one area where I'm tentatively learning. I don't think I've found training wheels yet. Boundaries are about protecting and valuing yourself. It's about knowing yourself and how much you can give. It's about putting yourself first and not thinking that it's selfish. For me, it's about not letting people drain all my energy, and not allowing others' opinions devalue my own. It's about knowing what I want to do without being influenced by others to do what they want me to do. It's about sticking to my creative plans and not letting negativity affect or diminish me.

I suck at boundaries with most people, but I'm improving. With Kim, I've found someone I can be honest with (and practice on). While we were working on this book, I struggled with multi-tasking. I have a day job that needs priority, and writing is slotted around it. One day, I received a message from Kim and my brain almost exploded. While I was writing, she was multi-tasking and had a pile of marketing ideas. I wrote back, *"Sorry, I'm head down, bum up, and writing. I can't focus on all those things now, but I'm with you 100% on whatever you decide. When I get this written, I'll be in a different headspace."* I felt awful, almost sick, after I pressed send. The guilt at not being able to do all of what she was doing was overwhelming, and I wanted to drop my jobs and talk with her, but I had my priorities. I was in a dilemma. She wrote back, *"LOL! I know what you're doing, keep writing."* The relief was instantaneous. She knew my one-focused self. She recognized my boundary and respected it. It was an incredible moment. My process was recognized as was the need for me to honor my process.

Allocating time to write is creating and enforcing a boundary. Writing your story from the heart is another boundary you're setting. Every time you stop writing to do something for someone else, ask yourself if it's necessary or are they not respecting your boundary; do they know your boundary. I still find it confronting to value what I do, especially when it's not my 'paying job', but writing is what I love; it brings me joy, and ultimately, it's what I want to do.

Looking after yourself, in all ways you need, is important for your physical and mental health. Good health is vital to power your creativity.

What do you need to be healthy – to nourish your body and your mind? Allow that to help fuel your creative writing energy.

MEDITATION IS SEXY

Kim

"With our thoughts we make the world." – Buddha

One way to access our creative higher-mind is through meditation. I know what you're thinking – meditation is nothing new and it doesn't sound as exotic or as sexy as the Tarot. But before you go jumping to conclusions, I'm going to tell you that meditation is extremely exotic and stone cold sexy.

How? I hear you ask. Great question. It is through entering the euphoric buzz offered through meditating that we are able to push through our inner boundaries to frolic with mysterious tales and visit enchanting worlds – and most importantly, we then allow higher messages to flow through to us that inform our daily writing. Is there anything sexier than that?

Considering meditation has increased in popularity over recent years, there may be a good chance you're already doing it, have tried it, or popped it on the to-do-someday list. If it's one of the latter two, now is the perfect time to *chillax* and get your Zen on.

The practice of stilling the mind has been around and exercised by our ancestors for centuries. And for a tradition to stick around for so long, obviously there must be something to it, right?

Apparently, the exact origins of meditation are subject to debate among scholars, but whether this spiritual exercise originated from the Dhyana, Taoists or Buddhists, makes no difference to us writers. It is in the here and now that we can reap the many benefits offered through the continued use of meditation, and where we should take advantage of this limitless well available to us.

While it comes as little surprise that many people throughout the world are keenly interested in meditating, only a few really understand its true purpose. Most of us are aware of the many benefits meditation provides. Research shows that when we meditate, our brain stops processing so much information. The frontal cortex goes offline, the activity in the parietal lobe slows down, the flow of incoming information in the thalamus reduces, and the reticular formation dials back the arousal signal.

What does this mean? – Loads of mental benefits. Meditation brings the brainwave pattern into an Alpha state that promotes healing and mindfulness. With regular practice meditation helps to:

- Reduce anxiety and depression
- Improve emotional stability
- Increase creativity, happiness, clarity and intuition
- Sharpen the mind
- Expand consciousness

But wait, there's more! The benefits of meditation are not only limited to our minds; our physiology undergoes a change too. Every cell in the body increases with more prana (energy). As our prana increases, so too do the physical benefits. Some of these include:

- Lower blood pressure
- Lower levels of blood lactate, reducing anxiety attacks
- Decreased tension in the body – eliminating headaches, ulcers, muscle and joint issues as well as easing insomnia
- Increased serotonin production that improves mood
- Improving the immune system
- Increased energy levels

If you know a little about meditation, the above examples are probably familiar to you. There's no denying the perks of the regular practice of meditation. Overall, stilling the mind reduces suffering on many levels, yet there is a higher, more valuable purpose to meditation that you may not know – It is through meditating that we strengthen our awareness to and begin to nurture our connection to the source of all creation, and thus open the portal to our higher-creative minds.

How perfect that you have this unlimited resource available at your fingertips!

I know that the prospect of meditation can be discouraging at times. Often, it can be difficult to calm your mind, stop the thoughts and get into a space that is quiet. I've been there. When I first started out, I soon gave up after a few tries with the assumption that meditation wasn't for me. I'm an INTP personality type, which means my mind rests at an almost constant stream of ideas and thoughts – to the point I often drive myself mad. Naturally, meditation was an impossibility for someone like me.

Not so. I did leave it alone for a while. A few years passed, until one day after studying some spiritual text, I dug my heels in. I found a piece of meditative vibes that suited me, grabbed my earbuds and set off to embark on a journey, determined to nail this baby or die trying. That's another characteristic INTPs possess – when the conditions suit and we're feeling it, an unshakable mindset can be our greatest asset. Although, I'm not sure my husband would agree.

Regardless of all things personality-driven, once I had decided to persist, nothing could stop me from my daily meditation sessions. Slowly I learned how to still my mind and release my soul to other-worldly dimensions. The invisible barriers parted more and more until I was able to enter the higher realms and succumb to the joy and peace those places brought, and I experienced the intensity of a love the likes of which cannot be fully articulated. There are no words enough to explain it to those who do not understand. Yet, for those that do understand, no words are needed.

I want you to understand. The higher realms can seem like an abstract notion – a golden mirage dangling like a transparent carrot you can never quite reach. Truthfully, I can understand the driving thought behind that assumption. There was a time that I may have considered something similar. But I am here to tell you that those other dimensions your physical senses are unable to perceive exist and are as real as the tangible life you are experiencing at this moment. Some would argue that those higher realms are more real than our physical world, but that's a whole other subject.

The main point and takeaways are this – through meditation we can raise our vibration. When we achieve a higher vibration or energy, we begin to disembody from our fleshy exterior, and still our mind enough to enter the great silence. This is where we can feel our connection to all that is and become aware of an intelligence much higher than any of us. When we begin to make the journey toward these higher planes, we begin to dissolve the invisible veil often shrouding our lives; we begin to reacquaint with our authentic selves.

This is where the magic happens. Meditation is like the springboard for your creativity. It is the place where limitations mean nothing and we open a current to receive information and messages, and act as a vehicle to a higher intelligence. This is where art has the ability to transcend art and is truly worth persevering through the sessions it may require to achieve a higher-state of mind.

Now that we know the value that meditation has on opening the pathways to our higher-creative minds, let's have a look at a few tips to get you in the Zen zone.

- Sit or lie comfortably. You may want to invest in a meditation chair or cushion.
- Close your eyes – or not. I prefer to shut my baby browns and see through the eyes of my soul.
- Choose a soothing or divine sound that resonates with you. I use the spiritual sounds mentioned in the book *Wishes Fulfilled* by Wayne Dyer. These sounds are based on I Am, That I Am.
- Focus your attention on the breath and on how the body moves with each inhalation and exhalation. Notice the movement of your body as you breathe.
- If your mind wanders, return your focus back to your breath.
- Meditate with a focus on creating a current with your creative resource. I will often ease into a session by repeating the mantra "I Am creative writing" or "I Am this pure revelation of everything I wish to know" – keeping my current work in progress in mind.

Meditation is where we find our sacredness and our truths, and with continued daily practice, meditation will help bring balance and clarity into your world as well as magic. As a storyteller, the world needs your magic. Get sexy and exotic with meditation and relish the beautiful experiences that abound in you. I promise you won't regret it.

MINDFULNESS; AS SEXY AS MEDITATION

Catherine

"Be where you are otherwise you will miss your life." – Buddha

I've known about mindfulness and I thought I did okay at it. I live in the present moment and I try to enjoy things with a child-like glee—or so I thought. Then I heard and saw someone who excelled at it ... and it blew my mind.

I'm emotional and sometimes feelings swamp me – negative and positive emotions. When this happens, my mind goes at a crazy rate of knots. Memories flood in taking me back to similar circumstances and events. I might then get multiple scenarios of *what if* as I play out a heap of options in my head. I go beyond *my* reactions and circumstances to include those of other people involved. I may project into the future and imagine what a changed life might be like, what else may now happen, and how things might work out for everyone involved. Amid the crazy, swirling emotions and rampaging thoughts, I try to survive whatever event it may be with dignity. Ha! I always end up overwhelmed and dignity flies out the window.

I thought this was normal, so imagine my surprise when my favorite sportsperson (I'm a sports tragic) was going through massive emotional circumstances—leaving the club he'd always played for, moving cities, getting married, and preparing for a grand final—instead of being overwhelmed, he focused his thoughts on the task at hand, whether that was packing a box, answering a question, or training.

Mindfulness in practice.

His composure made me realize how much I sucked at it. I had none of that mind control. I was struggling as I imagined what he was going through. There was no way I could focus on one task and not think about the future. Besides, as I did a task, I'd be wondering if it was the last time that I would ever do that and how I felt about that, would I miss it, would others miss me, etc.

I went out and bought Jon Kabat-Zinn's *Mindfulness for Beginners: Reclaiming the present moment – and your life*. I devoured it, learning many tools and techniques I had missed. There has been a lot of improvement but I'm nowhere near the skill level of my sporting hero. I can attend events where I would have been overwhelmed in the past, such as at a funeral. I now stop imagining everyone's life changing, stop imagining their sorrow, stop wondering how life will turn out, and stop pulling every memory of previous funerals and grief. I simply allow myself to feel my emotion in that moment.

This mindset makes a big difference to my writing. I focus on writing my story and doing the best I can, today, for these characters. I don't compare them with previous characters. I don't compare my writing today with yesterday, last month, last year. There's no projecting into the future, wondering if my publisher or readers will like my story. I keep my mind in the present moment, and the scene, or sentence, I'm writing.

Of course, I fail often. My mind wonders and wanders constantly, and that's okay because I notice it now and I know how to breathe and call my attention back to this moment. I like to talk to myself, mostly silently, so I might say, "Hey, don't stress about what your publisher's going to think; you've got to get the damn thing written first so let's focus on that now." And my mind laughs and focuses. If I'm lucky, I get lost in the writing and I'm totally nailing mindfulness.

For complete transparency, yes, I'm embarrassed that I've spent a chunk of my life not knowing how to control my own brain. I support an Aussie program that's trying to get mindfulness taught in all schools, so kids can learn these simple techniques to help them in life. I believe it's that valuable.

Mindfulness is about much more than helping with creativity. It assists with everyday life and helps me to navigate the stresses of living without getting completely frazzled and lost in looping memories and projections. If you're interested in the technique, there are heaps of apps that help by reminding you to be mindful.

MINDFULNESS IS STONE COLD SEXY

Kim

"The little things? The little moments? They aren't little." – Jon Kabat-Zinn

Mostly, I have always had a positive outlook toward life. I've always believed at my core that everything would work out for me – like an inbuilt faith mechanism. Do you know what I mean? I think we're all born with this inner knowledge to some degree. Think about it – it's an innate survival instinct to believe that no matter what happens, we'll be okay. It's as if we're aware that something greater than ourselves is watching over us, guiding us through our darkest moments.

Maybe it's a kickback from the realm in which we originate. Maybe the "Creative Source" or some angelic being working for the *Source* sprinkled us with golden dust before sending us off to dwell in human form. But not before serving us with a big dollop of amnesia.

Yeah, some hallowed being with crooked fingers and a cheesy smile dusted us and said, "Go forth, greenhorn; descend into the Earth and live your life with no recollection of your true self. That to rediscover who you really are, you will know joy and love, but you must also experience pain and suffering – but try not to worry too much because even though you cannot see or remember us, we've got your back. You'll be okay."

Sound like a viable scenario? That we were sent off from our divine origins dusted with amnesia and a side of faith?

Go on – roll your eyes and label me crazy, but it won't take away the pain and suffering that we all experience throughout our lifetime. Years ago, I fell into a deep depression that I struggled to escape. I had experienced bouts of the blues before when life seemed to get the better of me, but I was usually able to turn those burdensome feelings around and fight my way back to a better-feeling place. This time was different though.

The *black dog* gripped me during a time when I was raising my three children on my own. Something had happened that triggered me to spiral into a dark abyss. Every morning I'd awake, force myself out of bed and get the kids off to school, feeling utterly exhausted and devoid of energy by the time I arrived back home. Then, I'd curl up on the lounge and stay there for most of the day. I remember thinking that I'd never cried as much as during that time, and when I wasn't crying, I was numb.

This went on for a few weeks before I was able to step away from myself long enough to have a good look at what was happening. I was self-aware enough to know the power of thought, and that the process to feeling better meant I had to adjust my thoughts accordingly. One better thought at a time would supply the ladder I needed to climb from the depths of depression encapsulating me. Yet, I was so far down that it was nearly impossible to create and hold onto positive thoughts and feelings for any length of time. I knew then that I needed help.

I arranged to see a psychologist. I dropped my children off at a friend's place before attending these sessions once a week during the evening. I can't recall her name or how she looked but I'll never forget how she was able to help me see my situation in a different light. I'll always remember how she reminded me of the importance of mindfulness.

> *"Wherever you go, there you are."* – Jon Kabat-Zinn

She taught me how to train my mind on the present – that in any given moment to shift my attention to whatever I was doing and focus on that task and notice the simplicity of my actions. For example, if I was washing the dishes, I was to focus on the dishes and nothing else. She asked me to only think about washing the dishes – the warmth of the water; the way the glassware squeaked beneath the suds; the cleaning process.

Simple. Effective.

Those six sessions with the psychologist were enough to pull me from the depression shrouding my life. I learned that it was fruitless to fret about things beyond my control. I couldn't change the way others behaved, but I had the power to alter my own perceptions and reactions. She gave me the tools to curb my own thoughts from dwelling over a past that was haunting me, by bringing my attention to the present and focusing on now. Even through washing the dishes. Most of all, I learned how to appreciate the moments as they arrived – moments that I will never have again.

That is the point of being mindful. When we train our mind to be in the present moment, we free ourselves to make better choices. We can focus. We can dream. We can reach further into our higher-creative minds because we've allowed that space to breathe through the simple act of being present in the moment.

> *"The only way to live is by accepting each minute as an unrepeatable miracle."* – Tara Brach

I have encountered rough times since. I've struggled with personal matters through writing projects. It is when I can recall those simple instructions given to me long ago that I tame any urges to mull over and mourn past events or worry about a future that I've yet to experience. If every minute is unrepeatable, then every minute must be a miracle. By anchoring yourself in the present, you give yourself permission to fully experience your life as it unfolds. The more you practice this, the more you are filled with gratitude and appreciation. In turn, it is those unbridled feelings of gratitude that pave the way into dissolving the invisible barriers to your higher-creative mind. I love the way Wayne Dyer explained this concept when he stated, *"Change the way you look at things, and the things you look at change."*

It's so very true.

A Moment to Ponder Mindfulness:

Idowu Koyenikan said, "The mind is just like a muscle – the more you exercise it, the stronger it gets and the more it can expand."

- Considering your daily "thinking" habits, consider the above quote and techniques that you can use to strengthen your mind for expansion. Are there current situations in your life that could use a little mental tweaking?
- Can you think of a circumstance that may require a change of thinking on your part?

TIME-WARP & DREAMTIME: THE ANSWERS ARE IN THE PAST

Kim

Many of the ancient races to inhabit the earth before us were much more attuned to our connection to the universe and celestial forces. They worshiped natural divine deities based on a polytheistic belief system. It is surprising how tightly woven the invisible boundaries are that many choose to erect around their inner-world today.

Unhinge your thoughts. The universe is as mysterious as you and I, and functions in perfect divine order. Do you really think the universe exists solely to expand the blackness of space by creating planets and stars through spectacular explosions and great bursts of energy? That's it? Really? Seems a little fruitless. Perhaps the ancient races were on to something.

The ancient Druids believed the Earth itself was like the body of a dragon. They went ahead and built their sacred stone circles upon the "power nodes" of this body. They believed dragons connected us with the Earth's magnetism and healing waters.

The Egyptian conception of the universe centered on maat - a word that encompasses several concepts in English, including "truth", "justice", and "order". It was the fixed, eternal order of the universe, both in the cosmos and in society, and it was often personified as a goddess.

Kabbalah emerged during the Middle Ages – a Jewish mystical and magical system. Native Americans practice Shamanism: the shaman travels to the spirit realm to gain information regarding the community's needs like healing or spiritual growth. And we cannot discount the spiritual practices, traditions and beliefs based on the original teachings attributed to the Buddha – a set of philosophies sharing the goal of overcoming suffering and the cycle of death and rebirth, either by the attainment of Nirvana or through the path of Buddhahood.

I often wonder if evolution among the human race has actually declined over the centuries. Sure, technology has advanced us in leaps and bounds. We have access to anything we desire at a click or two, and our screens are filled with images of "the beautiful" people demonstrating the facade of what we ought to be striving to become. Our minds and lives are overflowing with constant stimulation. We have all of this yet it has come at the expense of losing sight of the universal energy that flows through our being and connects us to all that exists; it has come at the expense of losing touch with the real; the kind of real those ancient races honored and sought to worship – source energy, divine spiritualty.

There are many other ancient practices and spiritual beliefs that encompass the enigmatic nature of life and our universe, and through the ages those beliefs and teachings have seeped like golden nuggets of wisdom to guide and inform, and help us understand if we want to push past the chaos of the modern world and listen; and all that unlimited wealth begins by looking within rather than to the outside world. It's right inside you.

The universe, our existence, and the place we call earth comprises a series of wondrous miracles that occur in magnificent divine harmony with an energy whose sole objective is expansion, creation and ceaseless unconditional love.

How could we be so quick to disregard the unknown when you yourself are part of the great mystery? Psychic tools like the Tarot, clairvoyance, channeling or any other mystical practice really are not such a far stretch to believe when the foundation upon which we stand is riddled with a path of intricate beliefs, spirituality and sacred ancient magic.

Since the beginning of time storytelling has played a vital role in the evolution of humanity. It is no secret that storytelling originated through visual drawings, such as cave depictions and paintings, before shifting into oral traditions that passed down through the generations. It is through stories that we seek to learn about the world and the universe, and it also helps us understand relationships.

Dreamtime Stories

The Australian Aboriginal culture is one of the world's oldest cultures. Throughout the ages, this magnificent race of indigenous people has used Dreamtime to help them better understand the natural and mystical elements of our world, their people and their culture, as well as their history. Aboriginal children are told early in life about the structured and detailed stories embellished with valuable lessons about their elders' journeys and accomplishments. In turn, as their children grow into adults, passing the Dreamtime stories to the younger generations becomes their responsibility.

The Aborigines believed that Dreamtime was the very beginning, and that the land and the people were created by the spirits. They believed the spirits were responsible for creating all that existed, including their totems and their Dreaming.

Dreamtime stories are more than myths, legends or fables. These fascinating spiels are far from fairytales. They are the

Aborigines' accumulated knowledge, spirituality and wisdom. The storyteller's role is really that of cultural educator, channeling their spiritual Dreaming, which is demonstrated through visual art, oral storytelling, dance and music, as well as totems and lore. Together they form an all-encompassing mystical whole – The Dreaming.

Spirituality and Story

Aboriginal spirituality is deeply linked to the land. This ancient race of earthly worshippers believe that all objects are living and share the same soul or spirit as the people. A feeling of oneness, interconnectedness and belonging rests at the core of their beliefs. They learn to see with their "inner-eye" and view the world through the lens of their souls – which means there is no sense of separateness between the material world and the sacred world of creative energy. These relationships and the knowledge of how they are interconnected are expressed through their sacred stories.

While stories have been used to articulate the experiences and tribulations of our earliest ancestors to guide, teach and inform, and have existed to provide cautionary warnings to their predecessors, it also through storytelling that we have searched for the sacred dimension of life. We need to be ceaselessly reminded of the authentic nature of our lives, and we need our artistic inspiration to propel and transform those energies within and between us into messages that will continue to uplift and influence the generations.

It is well-established that when we raise our level of vibration, we attract influences from higher realms. While we don't know for certain where artistic inspiration originates, this wonderous resource is available to us all and is the cornerstone of all creation.

This is not a vague, mystical conundrum as many might think. In fact, just as the ancient race of Aborigines have practiced seeing with their "inner-eye", thus, connecting with the source of all creative energy to produce their sacred Dreamtime stories, similarly the higher realms are available to every human being.

It is at this higher level of the creative process that we become a transparent agent for another intelligence to pass through us. From this perspective, we receive fragments of intuitive revelations and become hosts to energies much larger than we are, originating from mysterious and spiritual realms. Simply put, God speaks to us through art; and I'm not necessarily talking about God in the sense of any identity espoused by religion, but that deepest sense of God in the formless existence of the eternal perfect.

All people of the world are offered this unique gift to increase our perspective of the human condition, and these insightful nuggets are often left behind in the form of works of art, including stories. The connotations of this phenomenon are significant. It is when artists reach into those higher realms to express deeper levels of the human experience that art transcends art and has the potential to help awaken something within us.

So, how as modern-day storytellers can we raise our vibrations and establish a connection to the higher realms and use those mystical currents to inform our own version of Dreamtime stories?

The answer lies in a time before our lives became a fast-track series of fleeting experiences and modern innovations – the past.

Dreamtime Story Tools

Ground yourself and connect with the earth. The Australian Aborigines believe in their connection to the land. Humans have always been in close contact with the earth, but our contemporary lifestyles have served to disconnect us from the earth's energy, making us more vulnerable to stress and illness. The Aborigines use the earth to recover wellbeing. By doing so, they pay attention to all four dimensions of our being – mind, body, spirit and land.

Aboriginal beliefs tied to the earth have been reinforced through modern research. Dr. James Oschman, biophysicist and pioneer Earthing researcher, states: "The moment your foot touches the earth, your physiology changes. An immediate normalization begins, and an anti-inflammatory switch is turned on."

Aside from the physiological benefits to get barefoot and dig your feet into the earth, connecting with earth's energy reminds us of our connection to the creative source energy. When we can quieten our thoughts, feel and connect with the earth, we can harness that energy to propel us through the invisible doors to higher realms.

Live from the Heart

Aboriginal spirituality is so incredibly diverse, but at the heart of their spirituality is an emphasis on caring and sharing. Being kind to others significantly improves our lives. I am not just talking about a polite exchange of courteous behaviour here; I am talking about the real stuff. Being authentic in every facet of your life, to yourself and those lives you touch along the way, creates a ripple effect from the inside out.

When we express love for ourselves and others, we are demonstrating love for all of creation. Practicing kindness and appreciation raises our vibration to a higher level, allowing the divine, eternal currents to flow through to us.

Release Your Dream to the World

The world needs its artists. Your Dreaming through story is a gift to the world that has the potential to change and uplift lives. By raising your own vibration and embracing the mystical currents and allowing them to flow through you and into your stories, you are helping to transcend the human condition into magical realms.

Like electricity flowing through wire. Only the zap is a remedy.

THE PENDULUM FOR WRITING

Kim

Can you relate to this scenario?

Imagine that the planets have aligned. The stars are twinkling and shining bright over your Muse. The inspiring energy of the waxing moon has fuelled your creative well and you are at the top of your writing game. The words are flowing – you idly wonder if fire could potentially catch your fingertips as you clank on the keyboard faster than a Bullet Train en route to Tokyo City. Hell, even the kids are cutting you a break.

Then, in the next instant, you're drawing a blank. Suddenly, your words have hit a brick wall, your characters are giving you the evil-eye and the stars have forsaken your muse for a glitzy night out on the town in Tokyo City. And you weren't invited.

Sound familiar?

I've been there – my muse has polarized me. Yep, he has ditched me for a night out in Tokyo to swing it with other writers while I desperately grasped for inspiration. Yet, I am a writer. I cannot wait around all day hoping he'll tire of the Tokyo glitz and come back to me.

These are the moments that define us as writers; when we

realize that we cannot always rely on the muse to get creative. So, we need a back-up plan. I'm going to share one alternative method that I use to tap into my higher-creative mind – the Pendulum.

Creativity takes courage. As writers, we yearn to tell stories; to express a sacred part of ourselves and share it with the world. When we connect to our natural creative resources, we are actually tuning into the unconscious part of our minds; this is where we discover the pathways that lead us to glorious realms - the highest part of ourselves that defines our existence – the obscure and mystic higher-creative mind.

As creatives we rely on connecting to those imaginative resources that linger in the unknown realms. Strengthening your relationship with these transcendental dimensions is key to allowing your creative energy to flow - muse or no muse.

Raise your Vibration

It is well-established that when we raise our level of vibration, we attract influences from higher realms. While we don't know for certain where artistic inspiration originates, this wonderous resource is available to us all and is the cornerstone of all creation. It is at this higher level of the creative process that we become a transparent agent for another intelligence to pass through us.

The higher the frequency of your energy or vibration, the lighter you feel in your physical, emotional, and mental bodies. By raising your vibration, you become more in touch with your higher self.

Practice Raising your Vibration by:

1. **Mediation** – as previously discussed, mediation has been practiced by our ancestors for eons. The fact that stilling the mind has increased in popularity is related to the many benefits' meditation produces as a holistic practice. Some of these nuggets include stress reduction, positive effects on emotional health and enhancing self-awareness. Yet, there is more at play here. It is when we are able to cease our thought-stream that we are propelled into the great silence; and this is where it's at – the portal to the higher-creative mind.
2. **Connect with nature** – ah, there is nothing like curling your toes between grainy sand or feeling the soft blades of grass folding beneath your bare feet. Don't roll your eyes and frown, because guess what? Getting intimate with the earth is like tapping into a natural reservoir of electric energy. That's right, the earth is equipped to absorb negative energy as well as supply what is needed to achieve homeostasis in our bodies. In short, stepping on the ground electrically balances you!
3. **Explore your inner-world through free writing** – free writing is to the mind what yoga is to the body. Allowing your thoughts to run free without restriction through your writing develops and fosters your writing abilities, as well as drives inspiration. In addition to promoting good writing habits, free-writing unearths emotional themes and can shatter those invisible barriers stifling creative expression.
4. **Contemplate your divinity and reflect** – without getting too enigmatic, it is amazing the revelations available to us when we take the time to ponder the

mystery of life and our connection to all that is. It is in the small, quiet moments when you're digging your toes in the sand and gazing at the ocean, or just sitting beneath the sun and appreciating its warmth that you connect with a higher energy, thus, raising your own vibration. Acknowledging and becoming aware of your connection to the universe cannot be underestimated.

The Pendulum for Creativity

Did you know that pendulum divination is one of the oldest processes for channelling guidance from the higher realms?

Historically, dowsing has been known for its ability to locate water, gold, oil and other minerals. Neolithic cave paintings have been found depicting figures holding dowsing rods, and the fact that dowsing was practiced by ancient tribes suggests that its practice is naturally occurring. But what dowsers use more than any other tool is the pendulum. While this form of divination is one of the oldest methods for receiving guidance from the spirit world, the swinging patterns of the pendulum can also be used to access our higher mind for creativity.

What is a Pendulum?

The pendulum is a very simple tool. It is a symmetrical, weighted object that is hung from a single chain or cord, and one that allows the user to tune into their intuitive powers. The pendulum acts as a receiver and transmitter of information, and moves in different ways in response to questions.

Pendulums can be made from all kinds of materials: quartz, crystals and gemstones. And metals such as silver, gold, coins, keys, and other objects, as well as various woods.

How Does It Work?

Much like the ever-growing popularity of current practices described for using Tarot to inform our writing, the pendulum can be used in a similar way.

Personally, I own two pendulums and use my favourite rose quartz pendulum daily to inform my creative writing, as well as to help guide me on other life matters. When using this tool to aid with my craft, I will generally consult on character elements and actions, and story structure and plotting. For example:

My muse is off in Tokyo and I'm stuck with a rebellious character facing a critical best-bad choice. I'm coming up with blanks. I might be in two minds about which way the story needs to unfold. I may even be reeling from the beats not making sense to me (even though I wrote them), and my thoughts are spinning – am I still in alignment with my story theme? Is this what my character would choose to do/say in this scene? Would she actually react that way? You get the drift.

This is the moment that I'm feeling somewhat confused with the progression of my story - you know, that part of the story where you feel as if you are losing sight of the global story?

Enter the Pendulum:

- Once you have your pendulum, it is a good idea to start by fusing your energy with the instrument. You do this by holding your pendulum in your palm and connecting with its natural-based energy. The next step is to introduce yourself to your pendulum. This might sound silly, but for you to get the most from your pendulum, you will need to get to know each other – intimately.

- Hold your suspended pendulum between your thumb and index finger with your dominant hand and proceed to the introduction. You can then begin with the basics and ask your pendulum to show you its responses. You're going to need to know the appropriate swinging actions for "yes", "no" and "uncertain" if you are to elicit information from your instrument.
- Ask for clarity and that your answers be given for your highest good.
- Take a breath and go ahead – ask your pendulum if your character would rather use a sword or a blunt object to slay her enemies! Or if your story is still on the right track.
- Love your pendulum. Accessing the higher realms is a gift. Always demonstrate gratitude for your pendulum and acknowledge these divine pathways your tool provides.
- The more familiar you become with your pendulum, the more accurate the information will flow through to you. In time, you will learn to trust its creative influence on your work and treasure the guidance and inspiration this tool can offer to your vision.
- Have fun! Honour your connection to the higher creative realms, but don't forget that your higher-self connecting you to the unseen dimensions does not take life as seriously as you do. So, get laughing as you access your higher-creative mind.

The pendulum itself is only a tool. Dowsers believe that they are contacting their higher-self, which is the part of ourselves that connects us to the universal consciousness, therefore has access to all information, including creative energy.

Using your pendulum to access your higher-creative mind and explore your ideas can be fun and informative, and is a great tool to use to connect with the higher realms, but like any other divination tool, it is important to remember that it should be used respectfully and for the right purposes.

Creative energy expressed through art has the power to transcend and shape lives. It is through accessing the mystical chords of the higher realms that we able to harness our unique higher-creative minds and share our gift with the world.

It's like giving wings to your dream and watching it fly.

WORKING WITH ORACLE CARDS
Catherine

"Three things cannot hide for long: The Moon, the Sun and the Truth." – Buddha

Oracle cards are simple to understand and use. The symbol(s) and/or word(s) are not multi-layered and don't usually need much interpretation or background knowledge. They're a beautiful way to receive a message.

There are many different types of oracle decks. They can be on a theme or a mix of words or thoughts. The themes for decks may include: trees, nature, animals, ocean, chakras, wisdom, elements, moon, feminine, sacred, empowerment, affirmations, insights, Druids, Angels, Saints, Mystics, Demons, Souls, time periods, light codes, Akashic records, gemstones, art.

My favorite Oracle deck is the Soul Tree Oracle. It's an 80-card deck created by Allyson Williams-Yee. She states the purpose of the deck is to facilitate guidance, inspiration, and assist with connecting to intuition. It's an intuitive deck to connect with inner wisdom; a visual representation of a person's spiritual journey. A sample of the Soul Trees Oracle Cards is in the picture.

This deck has 11 Interpretation cards—Awakening, Clarity, Guidance, Initiative, Inner Voice, Inspiration, Passion, Patience, Resistance, Risk and Stuck. **There are seven Chakra cards**—Root, Sacral, Solar Plexus, Heart, Throat, Third Eye, Crown. The other **62 cards are Soul Tree cards**. All cards have a beautiful tree painted in the space above the text. There is a small leaflet to assist with interpretations, but it's only a sentence or two. These cards require your intuition and mulling over the word on the card.

To use Oracle cards, begin with a few deep breaths. Sit comfortably, relax your mind, see what unfolds. Shuffle or fan the cards, or pick one/some, whatever you feel the need to do.

Here's an example of the Soul Trees Card at work. When Kim and I were thinking of this book, *Creative Writing Energy,* I asked the Soul Trees cards, "What do I need to know to help me with this book?" I drew three cards:

My brief interpretation of these cards is as follows:

BREAK FREE: This tells me to let my mind go, let all preconceived ideas go, don't conform, don't censor myself, break free of the 'normal' and get to the heart of myself. This is more what Cate does, and less what Catherine is like, so it was confronting, and challenging, to receive this.

1ST CHAKRA ROOT: I need to remain grounded, keep up health practices for my body. I need to connect to my higher/inner self when writing this book, find my truth, and be honest. The Root Chakra is blocked by fear, so I need to be fearless (lucky I'd been practicing with Cate).

INTENTION: I need to give writing this book my focus and set an intention (thought and action) for it to manifest (come into being). I need to ground myself well (the tree roots in this image are seen spreading out to support the tree), but I also need to allow my mind to flourish (the leaves and branches spread out in the image).

These cards pinpointed areas I needed to focus on to help this project be successful...or my examination of these three prompts was enough impetus for me to examine my weaknesses. Now, I can focus on minimizing my faults to move this project onwards. Whichever way Oracle cards work, this project has come into being, and I have been reminded of this spread often.

There's another deck that is also a favorite, the Celtic Tree Oracle. I use this deck for a more in-depth look or a seasonal read. Sharlyn Hidalgo is the creator, and although there are only 25 cards, it has a comprehensive guidebook with over 100 pages. The deck is based on the Celtic tree alphabet and steeped in Celtic cosmology. It's reminiscent of Runes and the runic alphabet.

The guidebook depicts each card and there are links to seasons and the lunar cycle; each card has northern and southern hemisphere dates (which I like, being in the oft-forgotten southern hemisphere).

There are keywords along with the meaning of the card in the upright and reverse positions. Each card has a lovely message directly from the tree.

To give an example of using these cards, I asked a similar question: "What do I need to know to help me with this book, *Creative Writing Energy*?"

I drew one card, 10. *Quert Apple*.

My brief intuitive read of this card: I saw blossoms and fruit on the pink/purple background, which made me think of a cycle. For my part in this book, I need to blossom and bear fruit. The background color reminds me of passion but also twilight; I need to quietly work at it, not be all ablaze. There's a tree in the image, so this is more than just blossoming and bearing fruit. I'm working on a small part of something bigger. As we've worked on this book, our plans have grown, which is interesting.

The guidebook suggests: The keywords for this card are female lineage, decision, choices, beauty, abundance, regeneration, fertility, motherhood. The *Quert Apple* is associated with the 9th lunation, Summer Solstice. In a reading, drawing this card suggests abundance, many boons and blessings, for which I need to be grateful. I also need to look at the paradise around me and do what I can to protect her. Healing and rest are offered. The messages from the *Quert Apple*: I represent variety, imagination, myth, choices. Choose with your heart and talents. Enjoy it thoroughly and fully, like that first bite of an apple, savor that before enjoying the whole fruit.

When using oracle cards, I've asked questions such as: is writing what I should be doing? With my current project, what do I need to know about this story? I've asked for help with characters and story development. I've asked for tips about where my story should be heading.

Even though Oracle cards are simple, don't always ask closed-ended questions and expect Yes/No responses. If you want to tap into your higher self, ask a question that provides the chance for a wide-ranging answer. You never know what's hiding in your mind if you're willing to explore deeply.

Sometimes I use Tarot cards and oracle cards together in a reading to give extra help with the interpretation. I often use my favorite Tarot deck and my favorite Oracle deck and they work together reinforcing the message. They may not have been simpatico at the beginning but they've grown together over time. Or maybe I've become better at reading enough into both cards so I get information cross-overs.

CRYSTALS AND GEMSTONES FOR WRITING SPARKLE

Catherine

"How you look at it is pretty much how you'll see it." – Rasheed Ogunlaru

I've been a collector all my life. I've amassed shells, rocks, soil, sticks, discarded nests, scats, and all manner of natural curios. Sometimes I'll see something in a shop, and feel the need to buy them, giving them a home with me or with someone I know. Beach stones, smoothed by waves and wind, have often landed in my hand. A collection sits on my desk and sometimes I need to pick them up as I write, fiddling with them as I think, sometimes even as I type or write.

A few years ago, I was having a tough time rewriting. I wanted something new to help me through this period. I wasn't sure what but I kept thinking about my birth stone, blue topaz. I've never owned any. I've never felt drawn to it nor identified with it in any way. Now, I couldn't get it out of my mind. I looked it up and strangely enough, some of the properties of this gemstone included communication and creativity. I thought I might buy something symbolic of my struggle to crack this book, but the jewelry was expensive and I hadn't become a best seller with this book yet, so there was no way I could afford to get ahead of myself. Then I found ETSY. That's a dangerous place, so don't go there. Actually, don't get into crystals at all because they're incredibly addictive.

I bought a necklace with a blue topaz drop of three stones—because I was on my third rewrite (little did I know it wasn't the last). My writing ritual became make a mug of tea, butt-in-chair (B-I-C), lift blue topaz, place on neck, write. When I finished my words, the topaz came off. Whether the stone itself had an impact, or the ritual, or my belief, I got that rewrite done.

While looking at ETSY, I was inspired by the gemstone jewelry, especially the wire wrapped stones. I knew people who could benefit from stones. Wearing them is so much easier than having them in your pocket (or bra) where they fall out (or you forget them until you undress and then you cause a racket that's not so easy to explain). I've become a twister and torturer of wire, wrapping them around stones, threading them onto adjustable leather necklaces, and gifting them to unsuspecting souls.

I have a small pile of positive-energy stones on my computer desk, catching the sunlight and sparkling. I have a few dark stones (obsidian, tourmaline, onyx, hematite) to protect me from negativity (mostly my own!). I have stones for healing, stones to wear, or just to hold or gaze on. Each morning as I dress, I take a moment to think about what color shirt I need for the day, and what stone I need with me (in my pocket, bra, or as a necklace).

Crystals, gemstones, pebbles, rocks, stones – no one needs to see them. No one needs to know why you have them. If carrying them or touching a piece of earth inspires you, use it. I do.

A List of Some Useful Stones and Their Properties

Stone - Properties

- Blue topaz - helps writer's block, inspires creativity
- Tourmaline - supportive, grounding
- Obsidian - self-aware
- Onyx - lets you breathe easier, release
- Hematite - energizing, vitalizing, grounding
- Sunstone - breathe life into creative spirit
- Malachite - tough love – unfiltered advice
- Amethyst - calming, intuitive, clearing mind
- Rhodochrosite - self-love
- Labradorite - spiritual connection
- Turquoise - path to your vibrationally highest self
- Blue lace agate - communication
- Fluorite - focus
- Smoky quartz - clears blocked energy
- Sodalite - self-truth
- Apatite - creative endeavors
- Carnelian - creative and confident
- Snake jasper - opens imagination
- Tiger's eye - strength, power, confidence, skills
- Jasper - calms nerves
- Agate - concentration
- Moonstone - patience, intuition
- Citrine - energy boost, confidence
- Celestine - clears creative blocks, opens mind

Don't limit yourself to this list. A crystal/gemstone addiction allows you to explore wildly, and with Google at your fingertips, a crystal life is easy.

USING TAROT CARDS TO EXPLORE THE MYSTERIOUS MIND

Catherine

"A few simple tips for life: feet on the ground, head to the skies, heart open ... quiet mind." – Rasheed Ogunlaru

I was taught Tarot was a wicked tool that foretold future events, so I avoided it for years. It wasn't too difficult because the traditional Rider-Waite cartoon-like depictions on the cards didn't inspire me.

Then I was given a deck of Angel Cards while I house sat for a friend – a fortnight when I intended to write a lot. The images on the cards were a bit over-the-top but as I read about them and looked at the pictures, I felt something. I began to use them, not to tell the future but to see what was in them and how they affected me. How could I use them?

Daily use had me realize that they asked me questions and made me think. I wanted to learn more. Months later, I met a writer who read Tarot through another writer friend, and I was gifted a Tarot reading. She used a deck filled with the most incredible symbols, images, and colors. Even through a video chat, those cards beckoned. I asked her what they were—The Mary-El Tarot—and later bought them for myself.

I own a few decks, and each has a different theme and feel. The symbols are unique, and not always the same for every card. I read intuitively, so I don't always get the same message from the same card in different decks. Tarot cards have become part of my day. I belong to a group, of mostly writers, who share interpretations and learnings.

The instigator of our group also creates spreads for readings, many of these focus on writing and creativity (You can find out more about Jodi's offerings at www.soullyrical.com). I don't use the spreads or cards to tell me the future; I use them as a tool to access my mind and gain a deeper understanding of myself.

How? Like art or music, the cards elicit an emotional response. They may create an emotion, or a word or phrase will lodge in my mind. My intuition takes over, allowing the symbols, colors, numbers, and cards to 'talk' to me. I pay attention to the quiet messages my mind finds as I stare and ponder. I know that sounds weird, but I've no other way to describe it.

If you're new to Tarot, let me give you a quick, Catherine-run-through (my brief attempt at explaining).

There are 78 Tarot cards. Twenty-two of them are called the Major Arcana. The rest are divided into four suits and are numbered. These are called the Minor Arcana. Different decks have different names for the suits, and they're often linked to the theme of the deck. The suits are linked to the four elements of fire, air, water, and earth. The card numbering takes the form of 1–10, and then the remaining have varying names depending on the deck, but they're often depicted as royalty—Page, Knight, Queen, King.

In the traditional Rider-Waite decks, the four suits are:

- Wands: depicting the spiritual (Fire element)
- Swords: depicting the mind and thoughts (Air element)
- Cups: depicting the emotions (Water element)
- Pentacles: depicting the body, physical (Earth element).

CREATIVE WRITING ENERGY

The four royal cards are:

- Page: indicates youth, learning, training
- Knight: adult, protector, warrior, not yet in control of all they have learned
- Queen: feminine energy, stately, in control
- King: masculine energy, planner, powerful, master of all he's learned.

The 22 Major Arcana cards are like a life journey showing you the gifts, skills, information, people, values, and talents that you may encounter along the way.

There are many books to help you understand Tarot more deeply. The one I found most valuable when I started was Barbara Moore's *Your Tarot, Your Way: Learn to read with any deck.*

How can you use Tarot cards with your writing?

Personally: Are you having a tough time making time to write, deciding what to write, wondering if you should write? You can ask the cards if they have any messages for you, and then select a card, or you could find a Tarot card spread that may ask the question(s) you're needing help with.

A simple and quick way to get inside your mind is to sit with the deck. Take a few slow deep breaths. Shuffle the cards while thinking about what you need to investigate. Pick a card, or a few cards, in whatever manner you feel is right. Have a look at the card(s); do they have any messages for you? Grab a pen and paper and start writing down your thoughts, without censoring.

If you need any prompts, start by looking at the color of the cards. What does the color remind you of? If you're into chakras, does the color correspond to a chakra or energy blockage? What symbols are in the cards and what do those symbols mean for you? How about the numbers; do they mean something? The suits? The run of cards/symbols/colors/numbers, if you chose more than one card.

Story/Character problems: You can do the same as above for problems and see what the cards tell you.

Think of one issue/character and draw a card. Does this give you an idea? Jot down any thoughts, see where your mind takes you. You can do this for any number of plot points or characters. You can list out plot points, or chapter numbers, and draw a card beside each one. Do you get any ideas, words, actions, thoughts from these cards?

I use cards to facilitate my intuition flow. I'm not strict on my usage and I often go with my gut when I'm reading. If you need more information, grab a Tarot book and look up what the card means. This can give you a deeper understanding or it may bring different ideas for your writing. If you want more help, I've seen writers offering courses and workshops on working with Tarot for Writing. Doing a course will give you many more ideas than this brief overview.

Let your imagination go. There are no rules. You don't even need to use what you come up with. Let your mind open and the words and ideas flow. Write it all down. You never know when something will strike you as perfect—exactly what you were looking for.

Here are two examples of using my Tarot Cards to help with character development (and story development too). I've asked who my heroine (main female character) could be.

I drew three cards from Beth Seilonen's beautiful Guardian Tarot deck. When I turned the third card over, I laughed. As a romance writer, a pregnant heroine is one popular way to conclude a story.

Let's have a look at how I'd interpret these cards (mostly intuitively, but I'll also give comments from the deck's guidebook). We have (from left to right, excluding the gorgeous box) the 9 Wands, Page of Cups and Ace of Pentacles.

The colors on these cards become more muted from left to right, so I immediately think that our heroine softens through the story, as well as blossoming and growing. Look at the lush leaves in the Ace of Pentacles, and the beautiful flowers and garden, with that gorgeous sky.

9 WANDS: This card has a strong red background and the face of the guardian is focused and almost devoid of feeling, but there's a sense of strength in that face. The leaves don't look real, they look like a mobile and not a tree. It's a very controlled image.

The Guidebook says that a calm and cool approach is needed, even if there's anger tucked inside. It says to deal with concerns before things get worse.

I'm imagining a rather headstrong woman who shows a controlled face to the world and deals with external conflict quickly and coolly, even if inside she's a seething mess of anger. She has an issue/hurt that she's hiding behind her icy façade.

PAGE CUPS: In the image, the person (or Guardian) is fleeing. The background is a beautiful sunrise/sunset, with a building/lighthouse alone on a clifftop. The card is both beautiful but isolated and alone. The figure looks sad, possibly distraught, but is holding that at bay while she runs.

The Guidebook speaks of nightmares that follow into waking hours. The ebb and flow of emotion inside. It speaks of keeping spiritual love strong and understanding that emotions may play at your mind when you least expect them.

Whatever is deeply bothering our heroine, something she keeps buried, is going to come back to haunt her and she'll need to deal with this. Some deep childhood issue? A teenage trauma? What can you think of?

ACE PENTACLES: Aces are new starts, beginnings. Pentacles represent the physical or body. In the card image, there's new life in the form of pregnancy, but there is also new life blooming in the flower the Guardian sniffs, and in the background.

The colors in this card are joyous and happy. Whatever besets our heroine, she's conquered the past and is ready to make a new life. Which is perfect for the Happy Ever After/Happy For Now required in a romance.

The Guidebook speaks of reflecting what has been (or can be) contributed to a better world. It asks us to consider how you can share your passion with others and move it outwards into the world.

Moving our heroine's new life into the world, makes this a bigger story. Can the change in her be a positive change for the wider community or world? Could she have some influence in changing something, maybe a law or a societal norm, that changes the world? Can her impact in the community bring healing to her? (I immediately think about the #MeToo movement, but other issues may include diversity, equal opportunities, families of victims, road rule changes.)

This time, I've used Marie White's Mary-El Tarot deck and asked the same question with a 3-card spread. I've drawn the Ace of Cups, 2 of Disks (another name for Pentacles), and 6 of Swords. My brief intuitive interpretation of the images in these gorgeously rich cards is below.

There is a comprehensive guidebook with the deck that is filled with information, but I won't use that here.

ACE OF CUPS: This card deals with the emotions, and since it's an Ace, it's symbolic of the beginning. So maybe my heroine's character arc will be about her developing feelings.

Maybe she doesn't know how to love after being orphaned and shuffled through foster homes and an orphanage.

2 OF DISKS: I immediately see the coins and wonder if she's completely money focused, driven to become rich because of her poor upbringing, and she has no time for emotion. She's out to win at all costs as long as she makes money.

6 OF SWORDS: This seems to be at odds with the character I've just drawn because this card is about helping others. How can I make that work? Maybe she's involved in something which forces her to help someone or something. Maybe she finds an injured dog and must keep it for a few hours until the vet opens (because she won't pay for an after-hours call), during this time, the dog works its way into her heart. Maybe then she discovers a poor family own the dog, the kids love it completely, but they can't afford the vet bills. She ends up helping them out but now the kids worm their way into her heart. She learns to love just when the hero vet needs to fall in love.

There are endless possibilities when you start asking and answering questions that spring into your mind from a random selection of cards. I'm surprised at where my thoughts take me, especially if I've initially looked at the cards and seen nothing. Digging a little and coming up with lots of possibilities can sometimes uncover mental gold. I hope that gives you an insight into how Tarot can be used with writing. If you're interested in Tarot, I hope you find a deck that inspires you as much as these two inspire me.

RUNES AND WRITING

Catherine

"Open the window of your mind. Allow the fresh air, new lights and new truths to enter." – Amit Ray

Runes come from the Viking period and consist of straight-line symbols depicting an alphabetical letter but containing a deeper meaning and energy. Traditionally runes were used for communication and as a means of self-enquiry (getting in touch with the gods). Runic symbols were originally carved into wooden disks or stones.

Runes can be linked to Tarot, I Ching, the Zodiac, the Viking gods, and Odin, the Norse god. They're mentioned in Anglo-Saxon, Norwegian, and Icelandic poems in the 13–15th centuries. It's believed that Runic masters understood the ancient, deeply spiritual meanings of the symbols but that the proliferation of non-pagan religions caused the loss of this knowledge. It wasn't until the 1960s that Runes gained attention outside of Scandinavia. They can be a bridge between the logical thinking mind and the subconscious. Since traditional meanings have largely been lost, runes work with modern interpretations and intuition.

There are 24 runic symbols, and a blank, in current rune sets.

They are carved into wood, metal, bone or stone. They're broken into **three Aetts**—*Freyr's Aett, Hagal's Aett and Tyr's Aett*. Runes are strongly connected to the elements—*earth, fire, water and air*—and are steeped in masculine and feminine energies due to their connections to gods and goddesses.

Runes are consulted by casting. They aren't easily used/read/learned because the pictures don't often conjure an intuitive response. If you want to use runes as a spiritual practice, or for assistance with writing, it may take time to get to know them, learn their meanings, and connect with them.

How to use runes with your writing

Some Runic keywords are: strength, prosperity, travel, partnership, happiness, womb, life force, growth, flow, stagnation, home, and death. You can cast runes and using just the keyword list, you may come up with ideas you hadn't thought of before. Your characters may use runes in the story to assist with decision making. Runes can be used as tattoos on your characters, or glyphs to help them find something, especially if you're writing a paranormal or historical mystery. Runes were mentioned in Tolkien's *Lord of the Rings*, as implements of power.

Runes may help with character name choices. Each Runic symbol is related to an alphabetical letter. A cast may help you form a name, or you may use the meaning of a rune to find a character's name, or even occupation, favorite color, tree, even birth month.

On Instagram I follow Stephen Aidan (@awitchespath), who's been doing a lovely series on runes. He has some great suggestions for working with them. The rune Ansuz (see Rune chart at the end of chapter) is associated with words, communication, inspiration, and clear vision. He suggests clearing writers' block by doodling the Ansuz symbol on a blank page, breathing slowly, and then writing without thought. If you like to write with a candle burning, a yellow or orange candle with the Ansuz rune etched into the wax may help inspire you. If you're looking for more runic information, he has many brilliant tips and hints on his Instagram feed. He also recommended a new book, *Living Runes: Theory and Practice of Norse Divination* by Galina Krasskova.

Many years ago, I made my own runes and these are what I still use. They're disks of wood I cut with a saw, and drew each symbol in pencil. I planned to burn them in, but have never felt the need.

Here's an example of a cast and how runes may assist with your writing. I shook runes from my bag asking for a story idea. Nine disks came out.

Runic Symbol	Name	Keyword
ᛒ	Beorc	growth
ᛏ	Nyd	need/necessity
BLANK		not yet known
ᛗ	Mannaz	human being
ᛡ	Ger	harvest/year/cycle
X	Gyfu	gift/partnership
I	Is	ice/standstill
ᛋ	Sigel	sun/life force
ᚢ	Ur	strength

What can you come up with for a story given these prompts? This is my brainstorm: A female character needs to grow because of some yet unknown reason. This growth is related to a man and may take a year. Maybe he's a farmer with the harvest linked to the Ger rune. Maybe she invests in his failing farm or they're an unlikely partnership after being gifted a farm. But they'll come to a standstill; maybe her emotions will freeze and she'll have to find a way to work on loving herself before she can love him. She's helped by the sun (or maybe he has a son, or she does). Something compels her to change, and in the end, their partnership brings great strength, stability, and a new life to them all.

Of course that brainstorm needs to be fleshed out and decisions need to be made, but if you've got nothing and you need somewhere to start, a rune cast has the ball rolling. Grab some of the ideas, or keep thinking, and hopefully your imagination will take over and a story will grab you.

Writing isn't all fun and magic, there's sweat and hard work involved too. Don't expect tools to do all the hard work. These tools may inspire, spark ideas, and allow you to think differently, but you'll still have to do the B-I-C and write the story. While you're doing that, I hope you find joy and enchantment, with moments of fun and delight, because writing is a magical process.

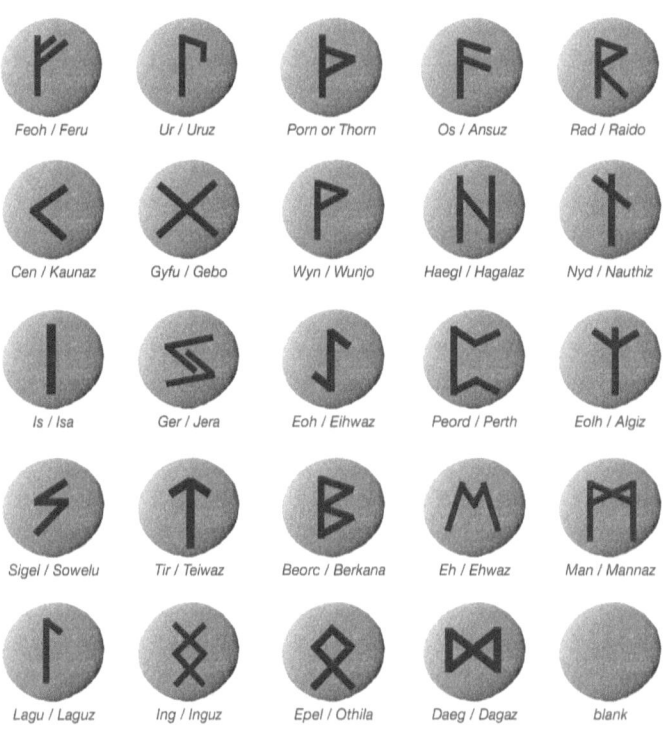

CREATIVITY IS LOVE

Kim

"It is passion, more passion and fuller, that we need. The moralist who bans passion is not of our time; his place these many years is with the dead. For we know what happens in a world when those who ban passion have triumphed. When love is suppressed, hate takes place. It is passion and ever more passion that we need if we are to undo the work of hate."

- Havelock Ellis

I used to be a little girl with a little room filled with nothing particularly girly. There were no pink mermaid curtains draping the windows nor were there white frills adorning the bed covers.

I loved climbing trees, riding bikes and erecting forts on top of the carport roof with my younger brother. Wrestling matches were fun too, till one of us was hurt enough to scream blue murder. I'll be honest, a lot of time that person was my brother. Those were the times when the fun turned sour and I shot dagger-eyes and mouthed terrible things that made him go crying to our mother.

Tsk. Mamma's boy.

Oh, brothers! There's a whole lot to say about growing up

with a little brother shadowing your every move. Almost three years separate my brother and me, and once upon a time he used to be smaller than me. But you know what? His lack of height had never stood in the way of his ingrained sense of protectiveness for me. He was loyal and courageous, and his love was fierce. I had seen that kid take on the meanest beefcakes in the name of love for me, and I always had his back too.

Although I would not have dreamed of admitting it at the time, my brother was my best friend, and for the most part, I adored hanging out with him. We spent hours creating new adventures and exploring unchartered territory as children. But sometimes, I had to retreat to a place of my own and turn my back on his pouting lips to leave him to his Matchbox cars. I had to shut the door to our room and delve into a world where he was not welcome or permitted. It was the delicate world of dolls.

Yes, dolls. Barbie dolls to be exact. I kept a bag beneath my bed filled with loads of Barbie dolls, one Ken doll, an assortment of accessories, and the biggest kicker of all – a Michael Jackson doll.

Every now and then, I needed to explore the soft feminine urges of the little girl I was and unleash my imagination with a focus on love.

Romantic love. You know, the kind of love that springs from your fluttering heart and inevitably results in the happily-ever-after? It is the type of love that captures your breath and steals your soul. It wraps around every cell in your body till you can't imagine a future without that person.

When you think about it, it is not so unusual that we begin to probe and delve into the beautiful mystery of love from such a young age, because it is love that governs your greater-self, your deeper-self. It is the part of you that connects you to all of creation, and this isn't something you can ever know intellectually; you can only *feel* and be *aware* of it.

Our view of the world is usually less tainted as children. Those magical years when our imagination knows no restrictions are also the years when our memories are the strongest, and our perceptions are most pure.

Somehow, we innately realize the knowledge that we are more than the flesh and blood peering back at us when we gaze into the mirror; we *know* that it is love from which we were born, and love that builds our whole existence.

Then time kicks in. The years pass and we settle into the dense 3D reality of our physical existence. We're bombarded with societal rules and restrictions, beliefs and religions, fear, hate and worldwide threats breeding the rancid contempt in the bellies of our leaders and spilling into the population. It is greed, materialism, brutality and murder, and the ever-present outcries of injustice constantly influencing and informing our worldview.

The veil thickens and the invisible barriers are firmly placed around our lives, leading to those moments when we forget who we really are. They are the same moments we get to choose if want to continue living beneath the cloak of ignorance or embark on a journey back to the real stuff.

From time to time the curtain will lift to reveal a glimpse of the eternal source gracing all that is. It's in those moments when you gaze from a mountain peak and your being soars with the beauty filling your essence; or those silent times when your soul lifts higher and you're encapsulated with a sense of unconditional love; or even a simple gesture from a stranger that touches your heart in a way you hadn't expected. However, most of all, it's in the relationships we experience with other people.

In her book, *A Return to Love*, Marianne Williamson says, *"In every relationship, in every moment, we teach each other love or fear."*

It is in demonstrating love toward others that we learn how to love more deeply. In exhibiting fear, we learn to be more frightened of life.

There exists one underlying force that connects us through our entire life. Despite the negative circumstances I mentioned above, humanity strives toward that feeling whether we realize it or not. It forms the basis in each one of our thoughts, interactions and tasks, it informs the words we utter and the way in which we see ourselves – *Love*.

Bold, fearless, glorious love.

It is love that forms the groundwork of most of our literature, art, music and drama, and love that has given birth to the endless inhibitions that humanity imposes on a false attitude toward sexuality – the most important expression of mankind. *Sex is really life expressing love.*

Love or fear?

You choose.

"In this relation between a man and a woman, in the sexual act, is expressed the complete physical, psychic, and spiritual hunger of being for another. No other activity or expression of mankind provides such a total outlet for love as the sex act."

- U.S Andersen.

When contemplating that statement, it's easy to recognize how little sex is understood, and how abused, particularly when we consider how readily available sex has become in our virtual worlds. We live in an age where voyeuristic perversions are fostered by the exploitation of sex. The overexposure of sex has had a significant impact on changes in our sexual behaviors and continues to influence our younger generations.

At the other end of the spectrum we face the age-old taboos and condemnation surrounding the sex act. This is when people get touchy and uncomfortable about sex, but how could such a natural and wonderous part of being human become saddled with shame, ridicule and immoral ordinance?

When love is present, there is no such thing.

Love is the recognition of our true selves – the motivation for unity and the desire for fusion. It's no wonder our stories are brimming with tales about love and romance. Even those authors who claim not to write romance are really writing some of the greatest love stories of all because it is love that flows from them and into their words; and love and passion, fueled with imagination, that embodies their creativity.

I believe every human is a creative. Every human can manifest and love; every being is ultimately cut from the same divine cloth. It's the golden threads that weave your heart and soul together and bond you with the universal energy – that brilliant light shining resiliently from behind every negative thought and experience that lets you know you *are* loved.

Love and creativity are one and the same. Love is the *source* of creativity.

Through all our experiences – the good and the bad – there is one profound and complicated sentiment that remains a universal thirst. One element is instinctual to our nature that is continuously streaming through the veil that blinds us from the truth. It is the invisible link driving us to a common basis – love and sexuality.

When I was a little girl, my dolls fell in love in the stories I created for them. Now that I'm a woman, my characters fall in love through the stories I create for them. I fall in love every day through story, my beautiful interactions with people, sacred soul connections I cherish, gratitude and the simple pleasures of life.

Love is more than a word on a page or a choice; love is fundamental to being human, and you cannot evolve, thrive and appreciate without it.

It is through our divinity that we are created by the source of love. It is through our humanity we learn how to express, give and receive love in our physicality.

When we look past the taboos, the abuse, and the exploitation of sex, and nestle down and really search ourselves within, we can acknowledge and celebrate the magnificence of sexuality and all its forms of expression. In his wonderful book *Three Magic Words*, U.S. Andersen articulates this perfectly when he states, *"The end of the sex act is not procreation – it is the expression of love!"*

Free yourself. Love yourself. Express yourself.

CONNECTING WITH YOUR HIGHER CREATIVE SELF

Judy Sweeney

You often hear about people being in the zone. Painters being in another place, the paintbrush seeming to have a mind of its own; musicians so engrossed in the music they are creating. You only have to look at some of the great guitarists to see what I mean; writers sitting at the keyboard for hours without a break, not wanting to stop because the words just keep coming.

If only it was like that all of the time. Alas, that is not always how it is. Sometimes, we just sit and look at the screen, the empty sheet music page or canvas and nothing flows.

I am not a writer, artist or musician. I am a Clairvoyant and, in my work, I have to go to my highest self and above every time I connect to Spirit. The principals are the same. The following are some of the practices I use to centre and reconnect to my higher creative self.

- Drink water, without hydration you cannot work to your highest potential.
- Breathe. The breath is one of the most important and

easiest tools we can use to open to our highest creative self.

Close your eyes and take in a deep breath, breathing in through your crown and into your heart.

Take another deep breath, in through your feet and into your heart.

Take another deep breath in of love from the universe and feel your heart expand.

Breathe in love from the earth and feel your heart expand.

Breathe in the I AM love from the universe into your heart, breathe in the I AM love from the earth into your heart.

Feel your heart expand, the energy in your heart is your creative essence, let it expand.

Feel the love for the I AM self that is you, feel it, sit with it, be one with it and allow it to expand and flow through you to every cell of your being.

Opening your eyes when you are ready.

Affirmations are such a wonderful way of instilling self-belief.

- *I am a Creative Being*
- *I know who I am and I know how I serve*
- *I am open to my joy*
- *I am peace and allow my joy to flow*

Acknowledging Blocks. We can't change what we don't acknowledge. I also believe that we can change something by looking at the emotion that you are feeling. Sit with it, bring it into your heart, not your mind.

- How does it feel?
- What emotion are you experiencing?

Fear, anger, frustration, not good enough, fraud? All emotions are valid, even it they are not real. i.e. you are always good enough etc.

Feel the emotion, hold it in your heart and say this until it lessens or goes away.

I CLEANSE YOU. I CLEAR YOU. I LOVE YOU
I CLEANSE YOU. I CLEAR YOU. I LOVE YOU
I CLEANSE YOU. I CLEAR YOU. I LOVE YOU

Prayer or Invocation. I always use a simple invocation before every reading, or healing I do. You can do the same thing. It doesn't have to be a long drawn out prayer it can be very simple. As I work with Spirit, I always ask for God and the angels to be with me. You don't have to do that if you don't want to, but I will say asking your angels for help is one thing that you can do and the angels love helping you.

You can say something simple like:

"Thank you, angels for being with me while I write
Thank you, angels for helping me through this block
I call on all the Angels of Creativity to be with me today."

About Judy Sweeney:
Psychic Medium, Reiki-Seichem Master & Spiritual Teacher

Judy is a well-known Psychic Medium and Workshop facilitator who is now in the beautiful and tranquil Tanilba Bay, Port Stephens.

With the move to Port Stephens she will be concentrating more on her Reading and Healing work with a focus on Light Language.

Skype and phone sessions are available for my overseas, interstate and distant clients, or if you just can't get to me in person. Distances makes no difference to the quality of the session as everything is done with Spirit and your higher self.

With a quirky sense of humour and many years' experience, including reading at festivals, the Mind Body Spirit, New Age Shops and her private rooms, you are guaranteed a high degree of accuracy, empathy, integrity and confidentiality.

Judy's Website: https://www.lightworkerworkshops.com.au

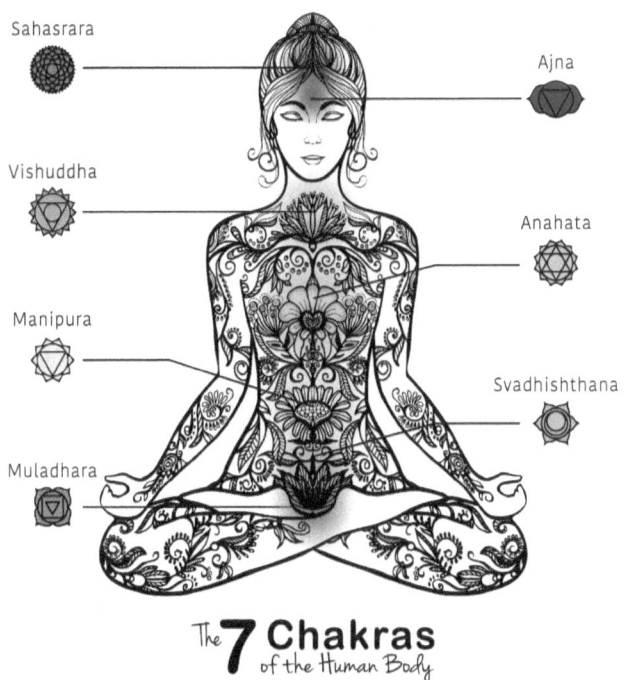

XAVIER EASTENBRICK

For those with electric soul-drenched dreams,
truth is more than what it seems.
Peer through the looking glass of a mystic journey's way,
looking toward tomorrow's destiny beyond the listless day.
Your yesterdays are fleeting zephyr clouds of dust,
and just as wind returns, so too the memories must.
Be wise in your words and every moment's start,
fear not the fool within who opens his/her passionate heart.
Remember the books you've read and what you've learned,
but understand true wisdom is experience earned.
What matters most is the energy we share,
a connected universe inspiring us to care.
Be sure to live a well-worn trail,
which if rich in love will never fail.
You begin from now, where it ends today,
tomorrow isn't just another day.
It is the dawn, the new, the starlight sire,
the exquisite blessings of a dream on fire.
Burn in the soul of your heaven's find,
and by quantum leaps within your mind.

CREATIVE WRITING ENERGY

The stars themselves are within your reach,
pinholes of light in the night so breached.
Open your eyes within and see
what life can be, need not be a mystery.
- Xavier Eastenbrick

Xavier Eastenbrick is a soul on a journey of life, meeting souls along the way. He adds to the richness of the universe and is grateful for each moment.

Pinterest: http://bit.ly/xaviereastenbrickpint
Twitter: https://twitter.com/eastenbrick

SOUL PURPOSE & CONNECTIONS FOR CREATIVITY

Kim

"There are no accidental meetings between souls." – Sheila Burke

t some point we've probably all contemplated our purpose during this lifetime. It is not unusual to find ourselves pondering the big stuff:

- What is my purpose?
- What can I share and contribute to the world?
- What is my legacy?
- How can I make authentic connections?
- What is my life's meaning?

Sound familiar?

It is logical that we reach a stage in our lives when we yearn for something more and meaningful—a time when we set out to seek answers about our world, our existence and soul purpose. In Maslow's five-stage hierarchy of needs, this self-discovery phrase of life rests at the top of his five-tier pyramid model in motivational psychology. Self-actualization is the process of realizing personal potential and self-fulfillment, as well as seeking personal growth and peak experiences. It is the desire to become everything we can become.

Creative writing is a soul-calling or soul-urge. I have yet to meet a writer to have stated otherwise. I mean, just look at what we put ourselves through – We choose to sit for prolonged periods at a time to slave (and sometimes procrastinate) over words.

It is like homework. To most people it sounds like tedious homework, and let's face it, sometimes it can feel that way. It is during those doubtful moments that remembering why you began writing that will help to bring you back to your truth. Your why. For what reasons did you begin writing?

I'm going to assume that you write books because your soul urges you to create stories to share with the world. Writing is a soul-driven occupation navigated by the wings of passion. Each writer is driven by an unknown force to create and release their messages to the world. It is through creating literature that we find meaning and purpose to our lives. It is through the creative soul connections we encounter along the way that we find ease and divine symphony as we fuse together to create for a higher purpose.

I have discovered so much about myself since I began writing. I can vividly recall the feeling that encapsulated me when I sat before a blank screen to begin writing my first book. It was like nothing I'd ever felt before – an acute rush of tingles and exquisite surges filled my being. It was as if my soul rejoiced in the moment. It was a confirmation that I'd finally discovered my soul purpose; my life purpose.

My writing journey has been a wonderfully fulfilling experience that continues to nourish and feed my soul. I still haven't stopped learning about myself, others and the world. Since I began writing, I have almost become a different person. What I mean is that while I had been living an authentic life prior to writing, the act of producing words has somehow reinforced and cultivated my self-perception, driving home my beliefs and values. Below I have listed some of the points that have come to light and/or strengthened within me since I have been writing:

- I am worthy of having a voice and expressing myself.
- What I have to say counts.
- To value myself as a writer, a woman and a human being.
- Not everyone will like what I create and that is perfectly fine.
- Not everything I create will work and that's okay too.
- To own my truth and be proud of those truths even when others judge.
- Living in fear is a life half lived.
- It is okay to give the kids a frozen pizza every now then. This will not harm them, and it doesn't make me a bad mother.
- Sometimes the tooth fairy is forgetful, but she always makes up for it the following evening.
- The words I create have power to uplift spirits an inch at a time.
- I can make a difference and I am strong and tenacious enough to keep trying, no matter what.
- Regardless of what I am working on, I have an unlimited resource of creativity available to me that I can access any time.
- Connections are important to soul growth and creating. I have learned to cherish, honor and appreciate those connections.
- I am not perfect and that's okay.
- People will appreciate and respect my imperfections as well as the honesty I bring to my work.

- Writing from the heart will attract the right audience for me.
- Believe and trust in myself and the universe.

Can you relate to any of the above? Do any of these points resonate with you?

Words are power.

Everything begins with words – our stories, thoughts, messages. Each word has its own vibration too. It is these vibrations that create the reality that surrounds us. Words create more than just stories; they inform our universe, our lives and our reality – and they teach us. Through creating words, I have managed to reacquaint myself more fully with my soul and to live a more authentic, love-driven and passionate life. In turn, embracing these rich inner layers will produce an unbridled fever that shines through my fictional and non-fictional writing.

Aside from the inner-growth, self-discovery and enrichment that your writing can bring to your life, we must acknowledge that our words can be extremely healing and enlightening to others. Too often we underestimate the power and importance of creativity. Therefore, there is a certain amount of responsibility that accompanies our work as writers. A certain amount of faith the universe has entrusted to us. This faith is also apparent within the connections that cross our paths throughout our writing journey.

We meet many people in our lifetime. They are here and they are there. Some are good and others are not. People cross our paths all the time, whether it be through social meetings and mutual acquaintances, work opportunities, meeting someone by chance at an event or some other scenario. They come and go, and mostly they may drift into the background of your past, barely summoning enough effort to be thought of again.

Then sometimes our paths collide with someone special – a

kindred spirit that seems to stir something deep within us as if our souls have known that person long before we encounter them. Perhaps long before this lifetime. Often, people will come together to create something profound and important. It is through these crucial soul connections that our own creativity is renewed and energized, which can bring positive change to the world.

How do we know when we've encountered a profound creative soul connection?

Have you ever met someone with whom you feel an inexplicable connection? Upon meeting them you may have felt an instant pull that defies logic or reason. Even before getting to know them, you sensed a special dynamic that you felt compelled to explore. I have been fortunate enough to have encountered a kindred spirit or two during my writing journey. These special people have come into my life for the purpose of collaborative creation and to produce change at a deeper level within myself. Personally, I think that is how you know when you've met someone crucial – you unite for the sake of creation and their presence in your life somehow evokes a personal change.

Meeting Catherine was like that. We met when I attended one of her workshops during the Wollongong Writers Festival. I remember looking over all the workshops on offer prior to booking. I was immediately drawn to Catherine's. I took notice of the underlying feelings that accompanied me when deciding whether to attend the event, and honestly, cannot fully articulate why, but I knew that something profound and important would result from attending. Specifically, there was a deep sensation surrounding Catherine, and that was before we had met.

Catherine is unlike anyone I have ever known. What I mean is that from the start it felt as if Catherine was someone I already knew before we even met. She was familiar to me. There exists a unique and special bond between us that we are both aware enough to recognize and appreciate. Our union has brought change to both our lives in positive and meaningful ways. The combination of us may appear highly contrasting on the surface – we often find a sense of amusement in contemplating our union. We think in different ways and our work is distinct from each other. Yet, it is those offbeat divergences that complement one another, and it seems to work. It has resulted in writing this book together; a title we are excited about because the topics are a shared passion. Moreover, we are honored to share the culmination of our connection to bring that positivity direct to you in the form of these words.

Keeping that in mind, let's look at some of the signs to be aware of that may signify a profound connection has entered your creative world:

1. They change you on a profound level. You will gradually sense that there is something about you that will never be the same. You may begin to feel a significant shift in your inner landscape that often reflects in your outer life.

2. The energy exchange that you have with a soul connection on a professional level will ignite your creative flow and bring a sense of "inner-knowing". In short, these connections will make you want to be a better writer and person.

3. They bring contemplation to your life and make you aware of the things you love and hate about yourself. These individuals will always mirror your own qualities. In the creative realm, embracing these qualities will bring more passion and integrity to your words.

4. You know that you won't forget them. We meet so many people over the course of our life. Our memories fade over time but soul connections cannot be easily forgotten. The imprint they leave on your soul, your work and life cannot be erased.

It is delicious, is it not? Soul work and life's mysteries. The most important thing to remember when it comes to our creative soul connections is that when it happens, you will know. Writing doesn't always have to be a solitary process. There is no mistaking the divine phenomena that exist when two souls come together to create for a higher purpose – you feel it all the way from your crown to the tips of your toes and it feels wonderful.

Therefore, the next time you sense something different or profound about someone you encounter along your writing journey, don't be too hasty to push it aside. Allow yourself to submerge in the feelings and sit with the current of energies and acknowledge your intuitive powers. It is often these special connections that reveal to us more about ourselves and begin to shine a light on the path leading toward our higher-creative minds. It's amazing what soul connections can help us to achieve as artists and as human beings.

A Moment to Ponder:

Thinking about your writing journey, write down some of the things you have learned about yourself along the way.

- How has writing empowered you or changed your life?
- What do you appreciate about the power of your words?
- What messages are you passionate about sharing with the world?

CREATION AND CREATIVITY: A RADICAL CHANGE IN PERSPECTIVE

Kim

"Looking at beauty in the world is the first step of purifying the mind." – Amit Ray

According to mystic philosopher Neville Goddard, creation is finished. Creativeness is but a deep perceptiveness of the entire contents of all of time and space co-existing simultaneously. In other words, all that you have ever been or ever will be exists right now. When we create, we are becoming aware of what already is. Therefore, creation is really the art of manifesting that which already exists.

Consider this statement pulled from the wonderful teachings of *The "I Am" Discourses*:

> *"There is nothing which comes into physical form which is not first perfected on the invisible or higher planes."*

Ancient and spiritual gurus have been aware of the concept of the time-space continuum co-existing in the infinitely eternal now for eons, and many of their teachings reflect this knowledge. **So, what does this mean and how can we use this information in our endeavor to create our stories?**

When we contemplate the notion of an eternal existence and that all events are taking place in the now, it requires a certain amount of shedding on our part. We must first unravel old thinking patterns, concepts and beliefs in order to comprehend the profound importance of this truth. We can then charge forth to accept a radical new idea – that there is a plane of awareness that you can opt to live at; an extraordinary space existing in the higher regions which you have the ability to access, and it is within these rich realms that we discover our higher-creative minds.

I love the way Wayne Dyer put it when he said, "You begin this exciting adventure of changing your concept of yourself by being willing to die to your present self."

Think about it; accepting that all things and events exist simultaneously explains the experience of that acute feeling of having met someone previously when meeting them for the first time, or even sensing that you've heard or seen a thing or a place before having experienced it physically. Some call it déjà vu while others recognize it for what it is – co-existing events strung along an invisible timeline.

As we go through the motions of navigating our lives, we experience and become aware of portions of what already exists. It is our self-concepts that determine the events that we encounter and experience along the timeline.

For the storyteller this is an exciting revelation. All those brilliant story ideas that have been vaguely sifting around in your head already exist; all you need to do is to become aware of them to bring them into fruition. We all have a creative fire that lives inside of us and is expressed in different ways. Our creativity is limitless and as discussed throughout this book, holds great significance when it comes to connecting to our authentic selves. By tuning into our higher-creative minds where the fire of creativity burns strong within us, we begin to nurture the path to self-discovery and connect in a more powerful way to our soul – and your soul purpose is creativity.

The scripts, alternative practices and tools offered in this book are intended to demonstrate the importance of your creativity and provide suggestions on how you can nurture this wonderful part of yourself. By lifting the mental fog long enough to access your higher-creative mind, you'll never find yourself out of a muse. Instead, you'll discover that you are all the muse needed to fuel the stories burning in your super-conscious mind.

We are born to create. Accepting that you are a deliberate creator brings a sense of inner-freedom and liberation to your life and experiences. Aside from your writing life, grasping and appreciating the flow of creativity can bring many benefits to your world. Here is just a little taste of how creativity can enrich your life:

- Strengthen a deeper connection with your soul.
- Provides an outlet for your emotions.
- Nurtures and strengthens your intuition.
- Promotes deeper passion, inspiration and motivation.
- Aligns you with your life purpose.
- Raises your vibration and energy.
- Helps to release stagnant and negative energy.

A Moment to Ponder Creativity:

Can you recognize how your creativity has impacted your life in positive ways?

Make a list as you think about it. Contemplating these positive effects will produce more of the same results and help to strengthen the pathways to your higher-creative mind and keep you uplifted.

AFTERWORD

Thank you for sharing your valuable time with us. The topics and methods discussed in this guide are subjective. Perspectives vary, as do our individual experiences as we navigate along our creative paths and lives. We were born to create and shine through creativity.

Awakening to the limitless imaginative resources available within us and nurturing these transcendental realms can make a significant difference to co-existing with our dreams and creating something extraordinary.

We hope you have discovered something new within these pages – something different that has wisped into your soul, resonated and triggered a sense of excitement; something worth further contemplation and exploration as you set about raising your vibration and diving into the rich layers of your higher-creative mind where dreams are for the taking and stories flow. This is the same realm that will uplift your energy and creativity, enabling your stories to make the world a better place.

Please keep in touch with us. We would love to hear if any of our suggestions have made a difference to your creative work. If you loved reading *Creative Writing Energy: Tools to Access Your*

AFTERWORD

Higher-Creative Mind, remember to sign up to receive our weekly Creative Writing Energy Prompts and Affirmations. Also, we'd appreciate your feedback in the form of a review at any of the online retailers where this book is available.

Thanks again, and don't forget to take a peek at the resource list for your reference.

Light & love,
Kim & Catherine xo

Resource List

Spiritual

- *Ask the Guides* by Sonia Choquette
- *The I Am Discourses* Volume 3 - https://theiamdiscourses.com/
- *Journey of Souls* by Dr Michael Newton
- *Messages from the Masters* by Brian Weiss M.D.
- *The Power of Awareness* by Neville Goddard
- *Wishes Fulfilled: Mastering the Art of Manifesting* by Dr Wayne W. Dyer
- Judy Sweeney - https://www.lightworkerworkshops.com.au
- Blair Stewart - https://www.blairstewart.com.au/

Science and the Mind

- *Becoming Supernatural* by Dr Joe Dispenza
- *Cure* by Jo Marchant
- *Diving for Seahorses* by Hilde Østby & Ylva Østby
- *Dreaming Through Darkness* by Charlie Morley
- *The Empath's Survival Guide* by Dr Judith Orloff

Crystals and Gemstones

- https://www.energymuse.com/about-gemstones
- https://julietmadison.com/the-power-of-crystals/

Health

- *Eat Feel Fresh* by Sahara Rose Ketabi
- *Medical Medium* by Anthony William

RESOURCE LIST

Mindfulness

- *Mindfulness for Beginners* by Jon Kabat-Zinn

https://www.smilingmind.com.au/

Meditation

- *Earth, Air, Fire, Water* by Stacey Demarco

https://www.headspace.com/meditation/kids
https://www.healthdirect.gov.au/meditation

Oracle Cards

- Celtic Tree Oracle Cards

- http://www.alchemicalhealingarts.com/
- https://blueangelonline.com/celtic_tree_oracle.html

- Soul Tree Oracle Cards

https://www.soul-trees.com/

Tarot Cards

- Guardian Tarot - http://www.bethseilonen.com/
- Mary-El Tarot - http://mary-el.com/
- Soul Lyrical Tarot Spreads - www.soullyrical.com
- *Your Tarot, Your Way: Learn to read with any deck* by Barbara Moore

RESOURCE LIST

Runes

- *Living Runes: Theory and Practice of Norse Divination* by Galina Krasskova
- *Runes for beginners* by Kristyna Arcarti
- Stephen Aidan - https://www.instagram.com/awitchespath/

Trees

- *The Hidden Life of Trees* by Peter Wohlleben

Feminine Energy

- *The Holy Wild* by Danielle Dulsky
- *Rise Sister Rise* by Rebecca Campbell
- *Sigil Witchery* by Laura Tempest Zakroff
- *Weave the Liminal* by Laura Tempest Zakroff
- *Woman Most Wild* by Danielle Dulsky
- *Women Who Run with Wolves* by Clarissa Pinkola Estés

Websites

https://www.hayhouse.com.au
https://www.heartmath.com/about/

- Maslow's Hierarchy of Needs – http://bit.ly/2xr6QWj
- Xavier Eastenbrick - https://twitter.com/eastenbrick

ABOUT THE AUTHOR - KIM PETERSEN

Kim Petersen is a USA Today Bestselling Author, author of The Ascended Angels Chronicles, and co-author of the Stone the Crows series. Her debut novel, Millie's Angel received a gold award in the 2017 Dan Poynter's Global eBook Awards.

She loves empty beaches, summer storms, big shady trees, and music - not necessarily in that order. Reading books is an obsession, and great movies and Netflix can be a satisfying pastime when it's time to tune out to the world. Mostly, she loves to ponder anything mysterious and beautiful.

Website and Social Media

- **Whispering Ink Press:**

http://www.whisperinginkpress.com

- **Website:** http://bit.ly/kimpetersen

  facebook.com/kimpetersen11
  twitter.com/kimpetersen_

ABOUT THE AUTHOR - CATHERINE EVANS

Catherine Evans writes rural fiction. She grew up in Sydney but desperately needed to move to the country. Catherine has a passion for rural life after spending eighteen years in agricultural research.

When life encouraged a career change, her love of creative writing came out of the closet. Catherine writes in two sub-genres of romance. She writes rural fiction because that is what she knows and loves, but there's a secret side too. Cate Ellink writes about sex and explores the shadows that society often frowns on.

Catherine and Cate happily co-exist on the south coast of NSW, Australia, but part of Catherine's heart belongs across the mountain ranges in the red soils of the flat plains.

Website and Social Media

- Website: www.CatherineEvansAuthor.com
- Email: catherine@catherineEvansAuthor.com

Cate

- Website http://www.cateellink.com

- Email cate@cateellink.com

- Facebook author page

http://www.facebook.com/CateEllinkAuthor

- Twitter https://twitter.com/cateellink

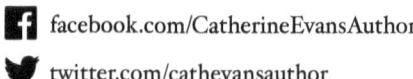

facebook.com/CatherineEvansAuthor

twitter.com/cathevansauthor

SIGN UP FOR WEEKLY INSPIRATION

www.ingramcontent.com/pod-product-compliance
Lightning Source LLC
Chambersburg PA
CBHW032044290426
44110CB00012B/940